Destination: Bethlehem

Dramas And Pageants
For Advent/Christmas

Anne W. Anderson
Nelson Chamberlain
Linda Buff and **Sharon Cathcart**
Pamela Honan Peterson
J. B. Quisenberry

CSS Publishing Company, Inc., Lima, Ohio

For more information about CSS Publishing Company resources, visit our website at www.csspub.com or e-mail us at custserv@csspub.com or call (800) 241-4056.

ISBN 0-7880-2332-2   PRINTED IN U.S.A.

Table Of Contents

Five Advent Candle Dramas

Advent 1 — He's Coming! ... I Hope

Advent 2 — I Can't Wait!

Advent 3 — Joy To The World

Advent 4 — Invading Force

Christmas Eve — The Party

Anne W. Anderson

Advent 1 — He's Coming! ... I Hope

Characters
> Dad/Father (mid-30s to mid-50s)
> Mom/Mother (mid-30s to mid-50s)
> Teenager (male or female)
> Child (male or female, age 6-10)

Running Time
> Five minutes

Synopsis
> The first scene depicts a modern-day family expecting someone who is coming at an indefinite time in the future. The second scene depicts a biblical family reacting to the prophetic promises about the coming of the Messiah. Both suggest the difference between a tentative "I hope so," and the sureness of "My hope is in ..." and raise the question, "Do we really want Jesus to come?"

Costumes
> During the first scene, all characters wear modern-day clothing, such as would be worn around the house on a Saturday afternoon. They should be barefoot or in sandals. During the second scene, the characters wear simple biblical-time robes over their other clothes.

Setting
> The living room of the home. A couch is upstage center. A desk with chair is downstage left. If this is being done in a church, a small pew can be used for the couch and a podium for the desk (Teenager would stand at it rather than sitting).

Props
> TV remote controller, hand-held electronic game, school books, small CD or tape player with headphones, vacuum cleaner, laundry basket, scroll, wooden bowl and spoon, dreidel

Scene 1

(As scene begins, Dad is sitting on the couch, flipping through the channels with his remote. Child sits on the floor nearby, playing with a hand-held electronic game. Teenager, with headphones on, is sitting at the desk, doing homework. An overflowing basket of laundry [which actually are the biblical costumes for the second scene] is by the desk. Mom is at the side, with a vacuum cleaner.

Mom surveys the scene, throws up her hands, and then turns the vacuum cleaner on. Dad glares at her and pretends to turn up the volume with the remote. Child jumps as if startled, but keeps playing. Teenager is oblivious.

Mom deliberately vacuums around Child — or moves Child — while Child continues playing game, moves Dad's feet and vacuums under them, and vacuums under Teenager's desk. Then Mom turns off vacuum)

Mom: *(Sarcastically)* I want to thank you all for your help today. *(She is ignored by all)*

Dad: *(Not really listening)* Yeah. Whatever.

(Mom shakes head, takes remote from Dad and pretends to turn off the television. She takes game from Child and removes Teenager's headphones)

Dad, Child, and Teenager: *(As each item is taken)* Hey!

(During next few lines, Child tries to grab game back from Mom)

Mom: Have you forgotten who is coming? This place is a mess!

Dad: There's plenty of time — we don't even know for sure he *is* coming.

Mom: He said he would be here ... and he always keeps his word.

(Mom hands game to Dad who puts it away and seats Child beside him)

Teenager: But he didn't say for sure *when* he would be here. I've got to get this report done!

Dad: *(Rising and going to Teenager)* When is it due?

Teenager: Tomorrow!

Mom: *(Knowing the answer)* And *when* was it assigned?

Teenager: Two months ago. But I've had so much other stuff to do ... and this is really, *really*, REALLY important!

Mom: More important than —

Dad: Honey, you're getting all worked up over this. Besides, didn't he say he would be taking us out when he comes?

Child: *(Jumping up from couch)* I don't wanna go!

Mom and Dad: *(Unison)* Why not?

Child: *(Grabbing the game)* 'Cause I didn't get to Level 5 yet! I don't want to go until I get to Level 5!

Dad: *(Going back to Child)* Now, Sweetie, you know you'll have more fun going with him than you will playing this.

Child: *(Suspiciously)* What kind of fun?

Dad: *(Uncertainly)* Well, I'm not sure exactly, but ...

Mom: *(Crossing to Child and trying to be more certain)* It's a surprise!

Child: That's what you said when we went to the Dental Floss Museum.

Mom: Well, that time I was wrong. This time, he's promised it will be more wonderful than we can even imagine ... and, like I said before —

Dad, Teenager, and Child: *(Dad uncertainly, Teenager bored, and Child sarcastically)* He always keeps his word!

Scene 2

(Hold poses from end of Scene 1 briefly, then quickly put on biblical dress. Ad libs such as "Have you seen my scroll?" "You might look by the window," and so on, will help keep the action going. Father is seated on couch from previous scene and is reading from a scroll. Mother stands at side, stirring something in a bowl. Teenager stands at other side and is combing hair [if a girl] or is eating something [if a boy]. Child plays with a dreidel on the floor)

Father: *(With meaning)* "There shall come forth a Rod from the stem of Jesse, and a Branch shall grow out of his roots. The Spirit of the Lord shall rest upon him ..." (Isaiah 11:1-2).

Mother: *(Piously)* The Messiah! I love hearing you read about the Messiah, may he come soon. *(Said as a cliché, without thinking about its meaning)*

Father: *(With feeling)* "... He shall strike the earth with the rod of his mouth, and with the breath of his lips he shall slay the wicked ..." (Isaiah 11:4b).

Teenager: How long ago did Isaiah prophesy that?

Father: *(Looking up)* About ... 700 years ago.

Teenager: So people have been saying this ... Messiah —

Mother: — may he come soon —

Teenager: — would come and save us for 700 years?

Father: Oh, no! Much longer. Why, King David himself spoke of it ... *(Turning the scroll)* Let me see ... ah! "I will declare the decree: The Lord has said to me, 'You are my Son. Today I have begotten you. Ask of me, and I will give you the nations for your inheritance, and the ends of the earth for your possession. You shall break them with a rod of iron; you shall dash them to pieces like a potter's wheel' " (Psalm 1:7-9).

Mother: *(Dreamily)* A thousand years ago, King David said about the Messiah ... may he come soon! The Most High was speaking through King David.

Father: *(Rising and going to Teenager)* You could even go all the way back to the Garden. After Adam and Eve sinned, they were promised that the head of the serpent would be bruised by the seed of the woman ...

Mother: That means the Messiah, may he —

Teenager: *(Sarcastically)* — yes, I know, may he come soon. But he hasn't, has he? Maybe he'll never come!

(Mother drops bowl and Father reacts in shock and horror. Even the Child looks around)

Teenager: Well, has he? I mean, how many times have we Jews been carted off as slaves to one country or another? *(Takes the dreidel from the Child and holds it up — see historical note at end)*

Child: Hey!

(Child goes to Mother to tattle. Mother hushes Child)

Teenager: Less than 200 years ago we weren't even allowed to learn to read until Judah Maccabee revolted. Maybe he was the Messiah! And now the Romans —

(Mother and Father try to hush Teenager)

Father: You must be careful what you say, Child. There are spies everywhere. Even Herod —

Teenager: Who isn't even a Jew!

Father: The Sovereign One has put him there for a purpose. It is not for us to question his will.

Mother: *(Disturbed)* Are you saying you don't believe the Messiah — may he come soon — will come?

Teenager: I'm not saying I don't believe in the Sovereign One ... or that he doesn't have a plan and a purpose. I just ... I'm just not sure about this whole ... Messiah —

Mother: — may he come soon —

Teenager: — thing. I mean, maybe he's already come and we missed him. Or maybe it's been different people for different times ... like Moses to deliver the Jews from Egypt ... or Judah Maccabee to deliver us from the Syrians. *How will we know who is the real Messiah?*

(Father and Mother are shocked into silence. Child looks at them both, then steps forward and looks up)

Child: May he come ... soon, I hope. *(Lights the first candle of the Advent wreath. After candle is lit, all actors exit)*

Optional

Choir sings "O Come, O Come, Emmanuel"

Suggested Scriptures For Further Discussion

Scene 1 — Matthew 24 and 25; Luke 21:25-36; 1 Thessalonians 4:13—5:11

Scene 2 — Isaiah 11:1-10; Psalm 2; Genesis 3; Matthew 3; Luke 4:14-30

Historical Note

During the occupation of the Jewish nation by the Syrians under Antiochus, the Jewish people were forbidden to read the scriptures and to teach their children to read. Many Jews did so anyway, but covertly, using games to disguise their activity. One of these games involved the spinning of a four-sided top called a dreidel or draydel.

Advent 2 — I Can't Wait!

Characters

Girl 1 (younger teen, age 12-14)
Girl 2 (younger teen, age 12-14)
Worker 1 (male or female, adult)
Worker 2 (male or female, adult)
Husband (age 30-50)
Wife (age 30-50)
Angel 1 (male or female, adult)
Angel 2 (male or female, adult)

Running Time

Three minutes

Synopsis

The phrase "I can't wait!" is explored from four perspectives. The first scene depicts two teenagers who can't wait to meet a celebrity. The second scene depicts two workers who can't wait for their shift to end. The third scene depicts a husband and wife who can't wait to be rid of each other. The fourth scene presents two angels commenting on the previous three scenes, and noting that what people really can't wait for is God's love.

Costumes

The Girls wear regular school clothes. Girl 1 wears or pantomimes wearing a watch. The Workers are blue collar workers — same color polo shirts and khaki slacks convey the idea of a uniform. They carry clipboards, and Worker 1 wears or pantomimes wearing a watch. The Husband wears a shirt, tie, and dress slacks. The Wife is more casually dressed. The Angels wear long-sleeved white shirts/blouses with silver lamé sashes tied diagonally from right shoulder to left hip, and dark pants/skirts. A female Angel can also wear a simple headpiece of wired tinsel with silver and silver ribbons hanging down the back.

Setting

No particular furnishings are needed. An Advent wreath with one candle lit — preferably earlier in the service with a reminder of the previous week's message on hope — is at center stage.

Props

Teen magazine, two clipboards, two shirts, small suitcase

Scene 1

(The sketch begins with everyone in position and their backs to the audience. The Girls are downstage right. The Workers are downstage center, slightly to the right and in front of the Advent wreath. The Husband and Wife are at downstage left and are turned slightly away from each other,

12

and the Angels are at upstage right. Angel 1 should be on the right of Angel 2. Hence the stage looks like this when the sketch begins:

Angel 2 Angel 1

Advent Wreath

Girls   *Workers*   *Wife Husband*

Audience

The Girls turn to face each other. They are looking at a magazine)

Girl 1: *(With a squeal)* Oooo! I can't wait to see *(insert name of current teen star)*. He is just so cool!

Girl 2: I'll just die if we actually get to meet him! I'm counting the days until his concert.

Girl 1: The days? Girlfriend, I'm counting the hours — 75 ... minutes — 37 ... and seconds — *(Checks watch)* 23 ... 22 ... 21 ...

Girl 2: *(Grabbing Girl 1's shoulders in excitement)* You're sure we're gonna meet him?

Girl 1: Yup! My dad is catering their party after the concert and he said we could help him.

(Both jump up and down in excitement and squeal)

Together: I can't wait! *(Sit down looking at magazine and freeze)*

Scene 2

(Workers with clipboards turn to face audience)

Worker 1: *(A bit disgustedly)* I can't wait until this shift ends.

Worker 2: Big plans for tonight?

Worker 1: Not really ... just been one of those days.

Worker 2: That's for sure — I can't believe how that order got messed up.

Worker 1: It wasn't anybody's fault ... and kind of everybody's fault. But stuff happens.

Worker 2: Yeah — and it all happened at once today!

Worker 1: It wouldn't have been so bad if the boss hadn't made such a big deal out of it.

Worker 2: I thought we'd never hear the end of it.

Worker 1: We probably haven't. And it's not like the world is going to end if this shipment of nails is two days late.

Worker 2: Kind of makes you wonder what the point is, doesn't it? I mean, is this really what life is all about? You get up ...

Worker 1: ... you go to work ...

Worker 2: ... you putter around the house or watch TV ...

Worker 1: ... you go to bed ...

Worker 2: ... and tomorrow you do it all over again.

Worker 1: Day after day after day. *(Checks watch)* Forty-five more minutes ... and 10 seconds.

Together: I can't wait.

(If there are steps at the edge of the platform, they can step down one or two steps and then freeze. If not, they stay in position and freeze)

Scene 3

(Husband and Wife turn to face audience. A small suitcase, opened, is at Husband's feet. Husband and Wife each hold a shirt)

Husband: *(Angrily throwing his shirt into the suitcase)* I can't wait to be out of here!

Wife: *(Also angrily)* Well, don't let me slow you down. *(Throws shirt she holds at Husband)* Here! Take this one with the lipstick on it ... that's *not* the kind I use.

Husband: You know, maybe if you were just a little more understanding of the pressure I'm under ...

Wife: As if I'm not? You try working all day long and then cooking dinner, cleaning house, and taking care of the kids ... with no help from you!

Husband: Don't give me that guilt trip bit again. *(Holding shirt in her face, but not realizing he's doing so)* I *do* work all day ... to make a lot of money so you can spend it on —

Wife: On what? *(Grabbing shirt and thrusting it in his face)* Lipstick? You know, I don't need you or your money. So you just go ahead —

Together: *(Bitterly)* I can't wait!

(They turn with their backs to each other and freeze)

Scene 4

(The Angels turn to face audience and survey the human scenes)

Angel 1: I can't wait until they let him rescue them.

Angel 2: They are pretty pathetic, aren't they?

Angel 1: *(Moving to the two Girls and stroking the hair of Girl 1)* Their young are kind of cute.

Angel 2: *(Following Angel 1)* Yes ... but it doesn't last long. They get caught up in idol worship so early ...

Angel 1: *(Moving to Workers)* Not even realizing what's happening ...

Angel 2: *(Following Angel 1)* ... and then wonder why life seems so meaningless.

Angel 1: *(Moving to Husband and Wife and sadly saying)* Then they turn on each other. They think they need things ...

Angel 2: *(Following Angel 1)* ... money ... or power ...

Angel 1: ... life to be exactly *their* way ...

Angel 2: ... to be happy. What they *really* need is life.

Angel 1: They look alive on the outside ...

Angel 2: *(Moving back to the Girls)* ... but on the inside they are dead. So that from the moment they are born, they start rotting away on the inside.

Angel 1: *(Looking at the Girls, but staying by the Husband and Wife)* Little by little ...

Angel 2: *(Moving to the Workers, but staying on the right side of the Advent wreath)* ... pointless moment by pointless moment ...

Angel 1: *(Looking at Husband and Wife)* ... until it is very evident on the outside. Why doesn't God just throw them out? Why do you suppose he even cares?

Angel 2: Only he really knows. I'm just glad he does care.

Angel 1: *(Moving to the left of the Advent wreath)* I guess that's what his love is all about — caring enough to give his life to something that should just be thrown out.

Angel 2: *(Moving to the right of the Advent wreath)* If only they knew ... they really can't wait —

Angel 1: — for love. *(Lights second candle of Advent wreath)*

Optional
Choir sings "People Need The Lord"

Suggested Scriptures For Further Discussion
    Scene 1 — Exodus 32; 1 Samuel 8; 1 Corinthians 1:10-25
    Scene 2 — Ecclesiastes 1:1-10; 8:10-17; 1 Corinthians 15:12-32; John 10:10
    Scene 3 — Romans 1:20-32; Ezekiel 36:26-27
    Scene 4 — John 3:16-17; 1 John 4:7-11

Advent 3 — Joy To the World

Characters

Bus Driver (male or female adult — no lines, but needs to be able to pantomime driving a bus)

Rider 1 (male or female adult, disillusioned with the world)

Rider 2 (male or female adult, represents God)

Running Time

Three minutes

Synopsis

A person riding a bus and reading a newspaper expresses disillusionment with the world, and wishes for some good news. Another rider, revealed as God during the sketch, shares the importance of taking God at his word — God's plan for bringing joy to the world.

Costumes

The Bus Driver wears a bus driver's hat and work clothes. Rider 1 is in casual, but professional, dress. Rider 2 is more professionally dressed than Rider 1.

Setting

A stool represents the Bus Driver's seat. The Driver sits on the stool facing sideways to the audience. Three chairs are lined up facing the audience to the right of the stool (so the riders sit subway or trolley style). An Advent wreath is to the right and upstage of the last chair. Two candles are already lit — preferably earlier in the service with a reminder of the previous two weeks' messages — that our hope is sure in all the meanings of the Lord's coming and that we really can't wait for his love.

Props

A stool, three chairs, four newspaper sections, large briefcase or satchel

(The sketch begins with the Bus Driver seated on the stool and Rider 1 on the middle chair. Rider 1 is reading a newspaper. Rider 2 stands in the audience at house right, checking his watch. Driver pantomimes stopping the bus and opening the door. Rider 1 should sway slightly toward the Driver as the Driver applies the brake. Rider 2, carrying briefcase or satchel, enters bus, pays Driver, and sits on chair directly behind Driver. As the Driver pantomimes stepping on the accelerator, the two Riders should sway slightly away from the Driver. As this part of the dialogue unfolds, Driver should react to the conversation by shrugging shoulders, nodding in agreement with Rider 1, and so on, while still pantomiming driving the bus)

Rider 1: *(Shaking head)* Sure is a lot of bad news in the paper these days.

Rider 2: What is it now?

Rider 1: More suicide bombers in the Mideast. Another CEO with his hand in the till. *(Turns pages)* Something else we can't eat anymore. And a bunch of kids who went for a joyride and ended up in a crash and burn. *(Folding newspaper)* Whatever happened to the good old days?

Rider 2: Good old days? Like when?

Rider 1: Oh, I don't know. Seems when I was younger — back in the '50s or so — life was better then.

Rider 2: *(Digging in briefcase)* Hmm ... think I have a newspaper from then. *(Pulls out a newspaper and hands it to Rider 1)* Here — you mean like this?

Rider 1: *(Reading aloud)* Korean War casualties number in thousands. A politician on the take. *(Turning pages)* Look at all the cigarette and liquor ads! And ... a bunch of kids who went for a joyride ... and ended up in a wreck. *(Folds newspaper up and hands it back to Rider 2)* Well ... I was just a kid then ... maybe I just don't remember the bad stuff. But Dad used to talk about how good it was when he was a kid ... back in the '30s.

Rider 2: *(Handing Rider 1 another paper)* Like this?

Rider 1: *(Looks at Rider 2 with suspicion, then reads aloud)* Rival gangs shoot it out in Chicago. Thousands homeless in Oklahoma. *(Turning pages)* Polio outbreak kills a bunch of kids. Japan invading China. Okay, okay. *(Folds newspaper and hands it back to Rider 1)* I get your point. I guess there's always been bad stuff happening.

Rider 2: Well, not always. Here — this is one of my favorites. *(Hands Rider 1 another paper)*

Rider 1: *(Does a double-take)* "God Does It Again — New Creation Completed in Six Days!" "Gardening Columnists Adam and Eve Share Tips" — page 5. What newspaper is this anyway? *(Looks at the top)* *The Celestial Times?* You are joking, aren't you? *(Hands it back)* But that's not the real world.

Rider 2: I admit, it didn't last long. But it *was* the real world. The one I intended.

(Driver and Rider 1 pantomime exchanging "He's crazy!" looks in the rearview mirror)

Rider 1: *(Humoring Rider 2)* So ... what happened?

Rider 2: The usual. One rebellious angel wants to run the show, two innocent creatures fall for his spiel, and the whole world is on its way to hell.

Rider 1: *(Moving over to empty seat)* I ... see.

Rider 2: Do you?

Rider 1: There's always someone who thinks he has a better plan.

Rider 2: And in this case?

Rider 1: Well, it's fairly obvious that Adam and Eve had it pretty good. But don't you think God ... I mean ... *you* were a little hard on them? It was only a piece of fruit.

Rider 2: *(Reflectively)* Isn't that what they always say ... "It was *only* a little bit ..." or "I was *only* joking" ... or — my personal favorite — "It was *only* once!"

Rider 1: But surely you didn't mean ...

Rider 2: *(Gravely)* That's what *he* said.

Rider 1: Who?

Rider 2: *(Looking way down)* You know who.

(Rider 1 looks down where Rider 2 has indicated)

Rider 1: *(Pointing fingers up alongside head like devil horns)* You mean?

Rider 2: Well, I don't know about the horns; but, yes, that's who I mean.

Rider 1: You mean he said you didn't mean what you meant?

Rider 2: In a manner of speaking.

Rider 1: So does that mean...?

Rider 2: It means that I mean what I say. Always. For all times. In all places.

(Rider 1 stares at him for a moment in disbelief mingled with fear. Driver stops bus, turns around, and actively listens to the conversation. As the rest of the dialogue continues, Rider 1 becomes more hardened and defiant. Driver uses gestures to question along with Rider 1)

Rider 1: So when you say that we are to love everyone ...

Rider 2: That means you are to love everyone.

Rider 1: No matter what?

Rider 2: That's right.

Rider 1: *(Holding up first newspaper)* Okay — what about Osama bin Laden *(or name of current world villain)*? How can I love him ... after what he and his cohorts have done? The thousands of people they have killed!

Rider 2: Once there was a man who made it his life's purpose to kill as many Christians as he could. He would drag them out of their homes and have them thrown into jail until they could be tried as infidels for blasphemy ... and then be stoned to death. He had the support of a whole religious system behind him.

Rider 1: And? You're not trying to give me some sugarcoated story about some maniac turning into Santa Claus, are you?

Rider 2: No. I'm telling you about what really happened — to a young Pharisee named Saul of Tarsus who turned to serving me ... and became my beloved Paul. *(Driver removes his hat)*

Rider 1: *(Agitated)* And you're saying the same thing could happen to Osama bin Laden ... or Saddam Hussein ... or —?

Rider 2: Are you saying it can't? *(Pauses)* Or that you don't want it to?

Rider 1: *(Rising)* Look, all I want is a little joy in the world ... a little *good* news now and then. *(Steps forward with arms crossed defiantly to just behind and slightly to right of Advent wreath. Rider 1's back should be turned to Rider 2)*

(Rider 2 stands and steps forward to just behind and slightly to the left of Advent wreath. Driver stands and comes closer to Rider 2. Driver bows his head and stretches his hand toward Rider 2)

Rider 2: And all I want *(Puts arm around Driver)* is to bring good news — glad tidings of great joy *(Lights third Advent candle)* to all people ... *(Puts other hand on Rider 1's shoulder — Rider 1 remains with back to Rider 2)*

(After candle is lit, actors exit)

Optional
    Choir sings "What Child Is This?"

Suggested Scriptures For Further Discussion
    Genesis 3; Deuteronomy 30; Isaiah 40; Luke 2:10; Matthew 5:38-48; John 15:9-17; 1 John 4

Advent 4 — Invading Force

Characters
King
Commander (commander of the King's armed forces)

Running Time
Four minutes

Synopsis
A king discusses the invasion of enemy-occupied territory with the commander of his armed forces. As the sketch develops, it becomes apparent that the king is God preparing to invade humanity and that the commander is the Archangel Michael.

Costumes
The King wears a crown and a royal robe over ordinary, casual clothing, and holds a scepter. The commander wears military dress uniform.

Setting
A high-backed chair on a small platform represents the King's throne room. Behind the throne (hidden from the audience's view) is a wooden manger and a scroll. The Advent wreath is downstage left. Three candles on the wreath should already be lit ... perhaps earlier in the service with a reminder of the previous weeks' messages — that our hope is in all the meanings of the Lord's coming, that we really can't wait for his love, and that he brings joy on his terms, not ours.

Props
A crown, a scepter, a high-backed chair, two report binders, a wooden manger, a scroll

(As the sketch begins, the King sits on his throne surveying the audience. The Commander, carrying two report binders, enters from the audience and bows to the King)

King: Do you have that report from the front, Commander?

Commander: *(Handing one copy to the King)* Yes, sire. For the most part, conditions remain unchanged. Rebel troops control most sectors with pockets of loyal forces scattered throughout. But ... *(Hesitates)*

King: *(Paging through the report)* Speak freely, Commander.

Commander: *(Beginning to pace back and forth)* Well, sire, some of those loyal to you are beginning to waver a bit. I don't know how much longer they can hold out. *(Opening his copy of the report)* They seem to be running low on supplies.

King: Are the supply lines cut off?

Commander: Oh, no, sire! Not on our end, anyway ...

King: Meaning?

Commander: Well, sire, I think some of our friendly forces are being worn down by enemy propaganda.

King: What kind of propaganda?

Commander: The enemy has spread rumors that you are not going to invade, sire.

King: What does that have to do with supply lines?

Commander: Our monitors indicate that because there's rumored to be no invasion, some of our friends are wondering why they bother to order supplies. So ... they don't.

King: I see.

Commander: *(Turning page)* Then there are others who have been sold counterfeit supplies.

King: Counterfeit supplies? Is there a problem in our warehouses? I thought I got rid of all the traitors there some time ago.

Commander: You did, sire. The problem is that while some of our friends are not ordering supplies at all and are just making do without — for a while, anyway — there are others who are requisitioning other sources.

King: There are no other sources!

Commander: Not for the real supplies, sire. But the enemy has set up supply depots that look remarkably like ours. Some of them even have our logos on them ... use our jargon. Their staff sometimes even wear our uniforms ... and their labeling is remarkably similar.

King: And what they offer is...?

Commander: Oh, it's definitely fake, sire. But it takes a while for that to be noticed. The change is so gradual that sometimes our people don't notice how weakened they've become.

King: So — many of our troops are barely holding on. And the rest of the territory?

Commander: *(Stops pacing)* Still under enemy control, sire. Each day there's more control over the population's thoughts ... which then affects their actions. This place is a mess, sire — degradation ... perversion ... cruelty ... despair ...

22

King: Joy?

Commander: Almost nonexistent, sire. The enemy has substituted happiness.

King: Love?

Commander: Even worse, sire. The enemy deflects what love gets through and turns it back on the population. Self-love has spread like the plague.

King: Hope?

Commander: *(Shaking his head)* Sorry, sire. Not only has the enemy propagated the rumor that you are not invading, they've also convinced almost everyone that you don't exist. Even some of those most loyal to us have bought the lie that you are only interested in destroying them.

King: If only they knew ...

Commander: Sire?

King: Sorry, Commander. I was just thinking ... if only they knew how true that is.

Commander: Your Majesty?

King: Not the way they think, Commander.

Commander: You mean...?

King: *(Closing his report and nodding)* It is time.

Commander: *(Taking a step back)* Sire! You can't be serious?

King: *(Laying report down)* I have never been more serious. *(Rises and lays his scepter on the throne)* My messenger, Gabriel, is already on his way. *(This refers to Gabriel being sent to Mary at the Annunciation)*

Commander: But ... but you will be the laughingstock of the enemy, sire!

King: *(Removing his crown and laying it beside the scepter)* No doubt. But how else will their defenses be penetrated ... *(Begins to remove robe)* except through my humility?

Commander: Sire, yes, their defenses will be penetrated. But that doesn't mean you will be safe ... or victorious.

King: *(Placing robe over the back of the throne)* Safe? No. Love is never safe. *(Picks up the manger)* But victorious? Oh, yes ... love is always victorious. They will be destroyed from the inside out ... completely and totally ... so I can live *in* them ... and they in me.

Commander: So, you are going to....?

King: I am.

Commander: *(Taking the manger from the King)* They will crucify you.

King: Yes.

Commander: *(Puts the manger down at center stage front)* They mean that much to you?

King: Yes.

Commander: *(Kneeling before the King and placing the report on the floor)* Let me go with you, sire.

King: *(Shaking his head)* This is something I must do alone. But *(Lays his hand on Commander's head)*, I have work for you here.

Commander: Whatever you ask, sire.

King: *(Handing Commander a scroll)* I have prepared a declaration. See to it that the messengers are ready at the appointed time and place.

Commander: *(Rising and brandishing the scroll)* They will be stationed at the four corners of the earth, sire, with flaming swords and full battle gear!

King: *(Putting his hand on Commander's shoulder to calm him down)* No, Michael. Only one contingency will be needed ... this time ... but make it a full one ... of our best singers.

Commander: Right! *(Does a double take slightly away from King)* Singers? Over enemy headquarters?

King: *(Shaking his head)* No ... to a field of sheep being watched over by a few shepherds.

Commander: *(Stepping closer to King)* I don't understand, sire.

King: You will. *(Places his hand on Commander's shoulder)* It will not be long. And my spirit will be with you.

Commander: Yes, sire.

(King leaves. Commander unrolls the scroll and begins to read)

Commander: *(As if reading to himself — reading some words aloud and others under his breath)* "Do not be afraid ... tidings of great joy ... city of David ... a babe wrapped in swaddling cloths ...

Glory to God in the highest ..." (Luke 2:10-14 NKJV). *(Looks after the King)* But, it's not a declaration of war! It's announcing a treaty *(Lights fourth candle of Advent wreath)* of peace! *(Exits)*

Optional

Choir sings "Thou Didst Leave Thy Throne"

Suggested Scriptures For Further Discussion

Genesis 3:21-24; Isaiah 45:18-25; Isaiah 64:8-12; Luke 2:10-14; Philippians 2:4-11; 2 Corinthians 5:18-20

Christmas Eve — The Party

Characters

Gabe (Gabriel — male, late teens to senior adult)

Mike (Michael — male, late teens to senior adult)

Man (Jesus — male, late teens to senior adult)

Person (male or female, late teens to senior adult)

Party Scene Characters (at least three and no more than eight total — male and female adults and children)

Running Time

Seven minutes

Synopsis

Guests arrive at a birthday party, but ignore the host, create chaos, and leave in anger. A different guest arrives looking for a different kind of party — a *real* party — and meets the host who, as the scene concludes, is identified as Jesus.

Costumes

Gabe and Mike wear white, long-sleeved shirts (buttoned, turtleneck, or long-sleeved t-shirts), dark-colored pants, and a silver sash worn diagonally from shoulder to hip. If Gabe and Mike are played by youth, they may want to spray their hair silver. Non-permanent hair paint can be obtained at a hair salon or costume supply house. Man/Jesus wears white pants, long-sleeved white shirt, and a silver tie, if possible. Person is barefoot (or wears old shoes) and dirty with unkempt hair and wears a dirty, torn, old coat that completely covers regular casual clothes. The Person has a trash bag tucked in a pocket. A plain white or more regal robe is also needed for the Person. At its simplest, the robe can be fashioned from a bed top-sheet folded in half top to bottom. Cut a V in the center of the fold for the head opening. Use white rope or decorative cording as a belt. Party Scene Characters wear Christmas party clothing — as casual or as formal as you like — and each wears a jacket or coat.

Setting

At one side is a tall stool on which is a party hat. Slightly downstage and next to the stool is a table with a birthday cake on it. Near the table (out of the way, but easily accessible) is a box of Christmas tree decorations. On the opposite side of the stage is a table (end table height and size) holding a baby picture (at least 8" x 10" framed) and a large baby album. Slightly behind this table is the Advent wreath. None of the candles on the Advent wreath is lit. Near the Advent wreath (out of the way, but easily accessible) is a basin and a second robe.

Props

Tall stool, one birthday party hat, table, one birthday cake (real or Styrofoam), end table, one 8" by 10" framed baby picture, one large baby album, one package wrapped in birthday wrapping paper, one large helium-filled birthday balloon on a long ribbon and weighted, several packages wrapped in Christmas wrapping paper and containing white elephant type presents, one artificial Christmas tree in a stand (with or without lights), box of Christmas tree decorations, trash bag, basin

(Before the service begins, the Person — in costume, although it should not be advertised as such — enters the church as a passerby who has wandered in and sits with the congregation. With the pastor's permission and without being overtly disruptive, the Person can either participate actively — although tentatively [fumble with hymnal, and so on] — in the service, passively watch the service progress with arms crossed or with scoffing gestures, or ignore the service by either pretending to fall asleep or pulling out a book and reading. As the scene begins, the Man sits on the stool at one side and holds a party hat. Near him is the table with the birthday cake on it. Downstage and on the opposite side is the table holding the baby picture and baby album. Near this table is the unlit Advent wreath. Gabe, carrying the birthday present, and Mike, carrying the balloon, enter)

Gabe: *(Setting the present on the table by the cake)* Hey — it's party time! *(Gabe and Man shake hands or embrace)*

Mike: *(Handing the Man the birthday balloon)* Happy birthday, sir!

Man: *(Shaking Mike's hand)* Thank you, Mike! I'm glad you and Gabe came by.

Gabe: So — how many years has it been now?

Man: *(With a grin)* More than I want to count!

Gabe: Seems like it was just yesterday ...

Man: Tell me about it!

Gabe: Okay — see there was this little village in this little country in the middle of —

Man: *(Holding up his hand)* — Gabe ... Gabe! It was a rhetorical statement.

Gabe: Oh ...

Mike: *(Looking around)* Where is everybody?

Man: They're on their way. You know how it is now.

Mike: Yeah. People do tend to leave things until the last minute. They're probably rushing around doing some last-minute shopping.

Gabe: Plus this time of year there are so many other things going on.

Mike: The kids have programs at school ...

Gabe: Grown-ups have parties at work ...

Man: Extra choir practice for the programs at church ...

Gabe: Maybe you should have been born in February — or July!

(Note: This part of the scene needs to move very quickly — think of the old silent movies where the action was much faster than normal — and should not take more than one minute total. Party Scene Characters carrying wrapped presents rush in from various parts of the church. One person carries the Christmas tree. The Person begins to show some interest in what is happening on stage)

Mike: I think they're here!

(The Party Scene Characters wave to each other, call out, "Hello!" "Good to see you!" "Merry Christmas!" and greet each other by name, as they quickly converge at the front. They ignore Mike, Gabe, and the Man. The Man sets the balloon down by the table holding the cake, then steps forward with his hands outstretched to welcome the Party Scene characters. He starts to say something, but the Party Scene Characters keep rapidly talking to each other, "How have you been?" "Have you heard the latest?" and so on, as they remove their coats and throw them in the Man's outstretched hands. The Man closes his mouth, shrugs his shoulders, and sets the coats behind the stool.

By the time he turns around, the Party Scene Character carrying the Christmas tree has set it right in front of the Man, hiding the Man, the stool, the balloon, and partially obscuring the table holding the cake. Others have rushed to throw the decorations on the tree. Mike and Gabe look at each other; then they move the stool to near the Advent wreath. Mike and Gabe stand at either side of the stool and slightly behind it as they watch the rest of the scene — react in increasing disbelief.

The Party Scene Characters set their presents down on the floor — anywhere, but not near the tree. The conversation becomes more competitive — "I get to put the star on!" "No, I want to!" and so on, as some quickly decorate the tree. The Man tries to join the party by adding a decoration to the tree or straightening one that has been thrown on, or by trying to shake hands with one of the guests, but the Party Scene Characters ignore him. One rushes to light the first four candles [not the center candle] of the Advent wreath — elbowing the Man out of the way to do so. A couple of Party Scene Characters quickly look through the baby album — after fighting over it, too.

Then all the Party Scene Characters pick up their presents and move toward the tree. The Man goes quickly to stand smiling beside the tree as the Party Scene Characters come forward with their gifts. Instead of giving the gifts to the Man, the Party Scene Characters give them to each other. The Man sits on the stool, shaking his head sadly as he watches the Party Scene Characters tear the presents open all at once and hold up the contents — which are inappropriate. They pretend to like the presents by smiling — not very convincingly — at each other, but then turn away and either mime gagging or laughing hysterically. As each sees what the other is doing, the Party Scene Characters become angry with each other. The Party Scene Characters grab their presents and their coats and rush out grumbling, "Some Christmas party that turned out to be." "Phooey on them!" "Bah, humbug!" and comments such as these. One Party Scene Character blows out the candles on the Advent wreath on his/her way out. The area is left littered with wrapping paper)

28

Gabe: What was *that* all about?

Mike: They didn't stay for cake.

Man: *(Rising and going to the tree to straighten an ornament)* I'm not sure they even knew I was here.

Mike: *(Rises and starts to go after the Party Scene Characters, hitting one fist into the palm of his other hand)* Just say the word, sir. I'll go get them!

Man: *(Trying to calm Mike down)* No, Mike. You know that's not the answer to ignorance or rudeness. They're the ones who are missing out on the real party.

Gabe: *(Comes forward to join Mike and Man)* I don't understand.

Person: *(Coming forward from audience/congregation area)* Excuse me, please.

(As this conversation begins, the Man moves to stand behind the Advent wreath. Mike stands with his arms crossed and turned partially away from Gabe, sternly looking after the Party Scene Characters who have left)

Gabe: *(Turning to Person)* Yes?

Person: *(Hesitantly)* I ... umm ... I heard there was a party here. Not the usual kind of party — you know where everyone is laughing ... but no one's really having a good time.

Gabe: Go on.

Person: Well ... I haven't been to a *real* party in such a long time. Someone told me about this one and I ... I was ...

Gabe: *(Gesturing encouragingly)* And you were...?

Person: I ... was hoping — *(At this word, the Man lights the first candle on the Advent wreath)* — that this really was a real party and that ... that ...

Gabe: *(A bit exasperated)* Go on.

Person: I was hoping that I could come to the party. But I don't have anything to wear — clean, that is. Everything I own is so awful.

Gabe: Awful?

Person: Most of what I have is torn and all of it is filthy. I mean — just look at me!

(Gabe holds Person at arm's length, turns Person around, and shakes his head in disbelief)

Gabe: You *are* pretty messed up.

Person: *(Hanging head)* I know. But the people who told me about the party said not to worry about that.

Gabe: Really?

Person: *(Nodding eagerly)* They said that the guy whose party it is — you know, the host — they said that he *loves* — *(At this word, the Man lights the second candle on the Advent wreath)* — to have people come just as they are! Can you imagine?

Gabe: *(Turns to look at Man, then turns back to Person)* I know someone who can. Tell me, why do you want to come to this party so much?

Person: I'm not sure I can explain it exactly. I've gone to a lot of parties because the invitations promised there'd be fun, fun, fun, and excitement galore.

Mike: *(Turning to listen)* And?

Person: They seemed like fun ... for a while. But then they'd start to be like when you're on a merry-go-round that's going too fast and you can't get off and all you feel is sick. And pretty soon everyone is getting sick all over each other — figuratively speaking, of course. *(Looks down at self)* It's not a pretty sight.

Mike: *(Picks up a piece of wrapping paper, looks at it, and says slowly)* No ... it's not a pretty sight. *(Turns toward Person and crosses his arms again)*

Person: I even tried throwing my own parties a couple of times — but they weren't any better. Anyway, the invitation to this party seemed so different.

Gabe: Different? How?

Person: The people who invited me didn't say anything about fun. But they did talk a lot about joy — *(The Man lights the third candle on the Advent wreath)* — joy that comes from serving others instead of expecting others to serve you. So I thought ... I mean, I hoped ... I mean ...

Gabe: Go on.

Person: I know I look a mess on the outside. And I'm really a mess on the inside. I know I don't deserve to be able to come to the party. But maybe I could just be a servant at it? *(Takes trash bag out and starts picking up the wrapping paper)* I could do stuff like pick up this trash here. And then maybe you need dishes washed?

Gabe: It's not actually my party.

Person: Oh. Oh, I see. *(Turns to Mike)* I'm sorry. I didn't know it was *your* party. Look, I'm really tired of fighting your invitations.

Mike: I beg your pardon?

Person: I don't blame you for being angry with me. I've thrown away most of the invitations you've sent — figured it was just one more scam I didn't need in my life. And I've been pretty rude to the people you sent to invite me personally. But you keep sending invitations and, well ... I'm tired of fighting myself ... fighting you ... about coming to the party. I'd like to have peace — *(The Man lights the fourth Advent candle)* between us. *(Holds out his/her hand)* Okay?

Mike: *(Uncrossing his arms and speaking gently)* That's not for me to say. It's not my party, either.

Person: *(Looking from one to the other)* Then who —?

Man: *(Stepping forward with his hands out to the Person)* Hello, _____ *(name of Person)*. I'm so glad you decided to come to the party.

Person: Do I know you? You seem familiar ... but I can't quite place ...

Man: *(Picking up baby album and handing it to Person)* Maybe this will help.

Person: This baby album?

Man: Read it.

Person: *(Opens the book and reads)* "Now in the sixth month, the angel Gabriel *(Gabe steps forward and bows slightly)* was sent by God to a city of Galilee named Nazareth to a virgin betrothed to a man whose name was Joseph, of the house of David. The virgin's name was Mary" (Luke 1:26-27 NKJV). But this is the Christmas story — oh! You're —

Man: *(Nodding)* That's me. *(Shakes his head sadly)* But that's all a lot of people know — or want to know.

Person: *(Putting album back on table)* I know I'm a mess ... but I really wanted to come and I'm so sorry I've been fighting about coming to your party and —

Man: *(Taking Person's hand)* I know. I heard. I'm glad you came. Come, let me wash your hands — *(Takes Person to basin and washes his/her hands)* — and give you some clean clothes. *(Takes Person's dirty coat off, puts it in trash bag, and hands it to Mike)* This can be burned. *(Mike bows slightly and exits. Gabe also bows slightly, moves Christmas tree in front of birthday cake and balloon, and follows Mike. Man puts new robe on Person)*

31

Person: *(Seeing birthday balloon and cake for the first time)* So that's what today is — it's your birthday party! But ... I didn't bring a present!

Man: Yes, you did! *(Takes Person to Advent wreath)* You have presented *yourself*, a living sacrifice, holy, acceptable to God. You "... walked in darkness ... *you* dwelled in the land of the shadow of death, upon *you* a light has shined" (Isaiah 9:2 NKJV). *(Together they light the Christ candle in the center of the Advent wreath)* I am "... the true light, which gives light to every *person* who comes into the world" (John 1:9 NKJV).

Person: *(Looks at Man for a few seconds, then says)* Happy birthday, Jesus.

(Person and Man freeze for two-second count; then exit)

Optional

After all actors exit, congregation sings — not too quickly — "Happy Birthday" to Jesus. This could be introduced by having the pastor, choir director, or a child light the candle on the birthday cake from the Christ candle on the Advent wreath and then inviting the congregation to sing. This could also follow the pastor's sermon.

Suggested Scriptures For Further Discussion

Matthew 22:1-14; Luke 7:36-50; Luke 14:7-14; Luke 7:15-24; Romans 12:1-2; James 2:1-13; Revelation 3:5; 22:16-17

Alternative Production Notes

This sketch can be performed two other ways:

Alternative One

To shorten the sketch, omit the party scene. The dialogue would then run:

Gabe: Maybe you should have been born in February — or July!

(The three look around and then look at their watches)

Mike: Maybe they're not coming.

Man: It wouldn't be the first time ... They just don't know what they're missing.

Person: *(Coming forward from audience/congregation area)* Excuse me, please.

Other changes: Have a decorated Christmas tree already set up at one side of the stage. After Gabe sets the birthday present on the table, he moves the Christmas tree forward and partially in front of the table. As there will be no wrapping paper on the floor to pick up, that gesture is omitted although the dialogue can remain as is.

Alternative Two

If you have a large congregational area, you may want to have more than one Person and divide the lines and action between/among them. Each would sit in a different part of the congregation and would react in different ways to the service.

Director's Notes

Director's Notes

_____

_____

_____

_____

_____

_____

_____

_____

_____

_____

_____

_____

_____

_____

_____

_____

_____

_____

_____

_____

_____

_____

_____

The Savior
Of The World

A Christmas Play
In Five Acts

Nelson Chamberlain

The Savior Of The World

Characters
  Voice (from offstage)
  Narrators (six in three pairs)
  Angel Gabriel
  Angels (one with a speaking part)
  Mary
  Joseph
  The "Little Animals" (young children in appropriate costume)
    Dove (two needed)
    Donkey
    Dog
    Cow
    Lamb (two needed)
  The "Little Shepherds" (older children)
    Jason
    Thomas
    Titus
    Simon
    Micah
    Nathan
    Lydia
  King Herod
  Wise Men (3 adults or children)

Music

A Youth Choir, Children's Choir, and an Adult or Youth/Adult choir can be used or a song-leader for congregational singing.

Setting

Bethlehem at the time of the birth of Jesus; also Jerusalem shortly thereafter.

Props

A stable that can double as a one-room house; a pallet, a small table, and a lamp or candle for Joseph; a doll wrapped up as baby Jesus and a manger for Mary; a "campfire" for the Little Shepherds to gather around; a spotlight or bright flashlight to shine on the Shepherds; Herod's throne; gifts for the Wise Men to present to baby Jesus

Prologue

(As the play begins, the lights are dimmed. The teams of Narrators are positioned left and right of the stage. The Youth and Children's Choirs are in place. Mary's house, a small, one-room structure

or painted backdrop, is to the right of the stage, unlit; Mary is seated inside. The Angel Gabriel is standing out of sight, offstage to the right. Joseph is offstage to the left. On the stage to the left there is a pallet on the floor for Joseph with a low table beside it, and a lamp or candle on top of it. A second Angel waits offstage, near Joseph)

Pastor or Play Director: *(From in front of the stage or off to one side)* Welcome. Many great and wonderful stories have been told over the years. Some are myths or legends, some are fables, and some are true. The story we tell tonight is not only true, but surely the most wondrous of all the stories humans have ever heard. There are other stories people would say have changed their lives, but only this one can change a person's life for all eternity. Listen well. Enjoy the children and enjoy the play. Our deepest wish is that this story will cause you to believe in the one who is not only the Baby in the manger, but also the one who is the Christ of the cross, the one who gave his life that you might life eternally.

Act 1
(A single, overhead light comes on to illuminate the stage)

Voice: *(From offstage)* The people that walked in darkness have seen a great light ... they that dwell in the land of the shadow of death, upon them hath the light shined ... for unto us a child is born, unto us a son is given ... and the government shall be upon his shoulder ... and his name shall be called Wonderful, Counselor, The Mighty God, The Everlasting Father, The Prince of Peace.

Narrator 1: In the beginning was the Word, and the Word was with God, and the Word was God ... He was in the world, and the world was made by him, and the world knew him not ... And the Word was made flesh, and dwelt among us, and we beheld his glory, the glory of the only begotten of the Father, full of grace and truth.

Narrator 2: Concerning this salvation, the prophets, who spoke of the grace that was to come to you, searched diligently and with greatest care. It was revealed to them that they were not serving themselves but you, when they spoke of the things that have now been told you by those who have preached the gospel to you by the Holy Spirit sent from heaven. Even angels long to look into these things.

(Gabriel steps forward into the light)

Voice: *(From offstage)* Gabriel ... It is time. You remember what I have told you?

Gabriel: *(Nodding)* Yes, Lord, I do.

Narrator 1: And in the sixth month after the angel was sent to announce the birth of John the Baptist, the angel was again sent out from God, this time to a city of Galilee, named Nazareth, to a virgin betrothed to a man whose name was Joseph, of the house of David; and the virgin's name was Mary.

(Lights up on the stage as Mary rises and comes to the front of her house. Gabriel moves toward her, startling her as he comes up to her)

Gabriel: Greetings to you ... you who are truly blessed! The Lord is with you.

Mary: But ... what ... why?

Gabriel: Please ... don't be afraid, Mary, for God has graced your life. You are going to have a child, a son, and you are to give him the name, Jesus. He will be great ... and will be called the Son of God, the Most High. The Lord God will give to him the throne of his ancestor David, and he will reign over the house of Jacob forever; in fact, his kingdom will *never* end!

Mary: But ... how ... how can this be? I ... I've never know a man. I ... I ...

Gabriel: Mary, the Holy Spirit will come upon you; God's own power will overshadow you. And so it is that this child that you bear will be called the Son of God.

Mary: Yes, but ... but ...

Gabriel: *(Smiling)* Think of this! Elizabeth, your relative, is going to have a child.

Mary: Elizabeth?

Gabriel: Yes, the one who is old; the one whom they called barren.... Mary, *nothing* is impossible with God.

Mary: *(Bowing her head)* Here I am then ... the Lord's servant. May this happen to me exactly as you have said it will.

(Lights down on Mary as she retires back within her house)

Youth Choir sings "Adoration" (or an appropriate carol or hymn)

Narrator 2: Mary knew that there were difficult days ahead: How would she tell her mother these things ... or her own father ... or Joseph, her husband-to-be? How would she explain? How could they believe? Mary visited her relative Elizabeth in far-off Judea. When she got there, the one who was to be known as John the Baptist leaped for joy in Elizabeth's womb and Elizabeth pronounced Mary to be truly blessed by God. Mary stayed there for almost three months ... and then it was time for her to return home ... and try to explain to Joseph the miracle of the coming birth of God's own Son.

Joseph: *(Walking out into the light at the left of the stage, upset and pacing the floor)* What am I going to do, Lord? What am I going to do? I love Mary, but I love you too, God; and I want to do what's right. I just don't understand. A child ... how can it be? I can't disgrace her in public ... but I can't marry her now either. Oh, oh ... I know, I know ... I'll get the two witnesses as the law requires and ... and I'll ... I'll break our vows privately. But, oh ... Mary ... oh ... *(Joseph stops pacing and lies down to sleep)*

Angel: *(Approaching Joseph quietly and standing back in the shadows)* Joseph, Joseph. *(Joseph stirs and mumbles, but does not awaken)* Joseph, son of David, don't be afraid to take Mary home with you to be your wife; for this child has indeed been begotten of the Holy Spirit. Yes, Joseph, Mary will indeed give birth ... to a son ... and you ... you are to give him the name Jesus, for he will save his people from their sins. *(Angel withdraws)*

Narrator 1: Now all this was done, that it might be fulfilled which was spoken of the Lord by the prophet, saying, "Behold, a virgin shall be with child, and shall bring forth a son, and they shall call his name Emmanuel, which means, God with us."

Joseph: *(Waking up)* Yes, yes, Lord, I'll do it, I'll do it! Right now ... today ... as soon as the sun comes up, that is. I'll go to her ... I'll ... Yes, I'll bring her home with me as my wife. And I will give him that name ... Jesus ... *Jesus* ... that will be his name!

(Lights lowered in preparation for the next scene)

Youth Choir sings "Come, Thou Long-Expected Jesus"

Act 2
(Mary's "house" becomes the stable with the manger inside. Mary and Joseph are inside the stable, Mary reclining, the baby Jesus in her arms; Joseph sitting by her side. The younger children, in their animal costumes, are gathered around the stable. The "animals" are very still, as if asleep. The lights come up slowly)

Narrator 2: And it came to pass in those days, that there went out a decree from Caesar Augustus, that all the world should be taxed ... And all went to be taxed, every one into his own city. And Joseph also went up from Galilee, out of the city of Nazareth, into Judea, unto the city of David, which is called Bethlehem, because he was of the house and lineage of David. to be taxed with Mary his espoused wife, being great with child. And so it was, that, while they were there, the days were accomplished that she should be delivered. And she brought forth her firstborn son, and wrapped him in swaddling clothes, and laid him in a manger; because there was no room for them in the inn.

(The sound of a baby's cry)

Mary: *(Rousing herself)* There, there, little one, everything's all right.

Joseph: Is he okay, Mary? Are you okay?

Mary: Yes.

Joseph: I can't believe it's happened like this. Here in Bethlehem. So far away from home. And us out on the road. Taxes! That's all these Romans think of. And no room, no room for us at all ... and after the angel came and told me about all the greatness of this child. No room. He turned us away ... that man at the inn!

Mary: *(As she carefully lays the baby in the manger beside her)* It's all right, Joseph. We're warm and safe in here ... and it's good to be away from the crowds. Surely, this is the right place for us to be ... in God's eyes.

Joseph: But the angel told you he would be a king!

Mary: Mm-hmm.

Joseph: I believe all that the angel said ... and yet wouldn't it be wonderful if tonight somehow God would give us a sign?

(Mary nods sleepily. Mary and Joseph draw even closer to one another and fall asleep. After a pause, the animals "come to life," rising, shaking themselves, gazing into the stable excitedly)

Dove 1: Look, so peaceful. Have you ever seen such peace?

Dove 2: Coo. Yes, the Prince of Peace has been born here tonight.

Donkey: The Prince of Peace? Here ... in a manger?

Dog: The Savior of the world lying in a feeding trough for donkeys and cows!

Cow: Why not? If he had been born in a palace, he would be a Savior only for rich men.

Lamb 1: And if he had been born in a house, they would have thought that this world was his home.

Lamb 2: Well, I think that it must be just the right place for him to be born.

Dog: *(Growling)* Sheep. I just noticed that there are sheep here. Are you lost? Did you run away? I'd better see that you get back to the fold.

Lamb 1: We'll go; we'll go. We didn't wander very far.

Lamb 2: But, somehow, I think that the greatest Shepherd of all lies right here in this manger on this night.

(Lights dim on the scene)

Youth Choir (or Soloist) sings "I Wonder As I Wander"

Act 3

(Seven little Shepherds — Jason, Thomas, Titus, Simon, Micah, Nathan, and Lydia — are seated together "out in the fields," at the left of the stage, "watching the sheep." At the back of the stage the angels wait in the darkness. Lighting for night scene)

Jason: I suppose that one of us ought to go and check on father's sheep.

Thomas: Right, Jason, so go do it.

Jason: Who, me? I did it last time.

Titus: No, you didn't. You made Simon do it.

Jason: What? You're crazy.

Simon: I sure did. I almost got scared to death by that strange noise I heard out there.

Micah: *(Making scary face and wolf sound)* You mean, like this?

Nathan: Cut it out, Micah. Don't pick on your brother like that.

Micah: But, it's fun.

Thomas: If it's fun to get scared, then go check on the sheep and *you* get scared.

Micah: Me? It's not *my* job. Besides, *he* offered to go.

Simon: Yeah, after you twisted my arm. *(Demonstrates)*

Titus: If checking sheep is not your job, then just what is your job, Micah?

Micah: *(After a moment's thought)* Being boss?

Nathan: You're not *my* boss!

Micah: Yes, I am!

Nathan: No, you're not!

Micah: Yes, I am!

Nathan: *(Emphatically)* Oh, no, you're not!

Jason: Stop acting like ... *children*. Someone ought to go.

Thomas and Titus: *(Together, pointing at Jason)* You go. *(Jason frowns)*

Jason: Or Lydia. Lydia can go this time. She never has to go!

Lydia: Who, me? I'm a girl! Dad would skin you alive if you made me go!

Thomas and Titus: *(Together)* Yeah, Jason, Dad told us to take care of her.

Jason: *(Muttering)* It's still not fair!

Lydia: Simon, I don't have to go ... out in the dark ... do I?

Simon: Of course not. Not as long as you're *my* little sister.

Micah: Right, just because she's *your* sister ... She's *my* cousin, you know!

Nathan: Sh-h! Don't be so loud.

Titus: Right, if our dads hear us arguing, they won't let us stay out here so late ever again.

Simon: Hey, this is kind of fun, isn't it?

Thomas: I'm glad our parents trust us, even if we do just get to watch the little flock.

Jason: *(Peering out over the stage)* Speaking of the little flock ... I only see eight lambs ... are two missing?

Nathan: They'd better not be! *Somebody* had better go check on the sheep.

Micah: Yeah, *somebody*.

Simon: Here we go again!

Titus: Ja - son ...

Jason: Oh, all right. I guess ... since I am the oldest ... and the bravest ...

Thomas and Titus: *(Together, sarcastically)* Right!

Jason: *(Walking off hesitantly, whistling as he goes)* Yeah, I guess ... I'd better ... go. I am ... the bravest ... and the ... *(Sound of wolf howl from offstage, prompting Jason to come running back)* Ah ... ah ... the sheep are fine. They're all there. You go next time, Thomas.

Simon: Scared, Jason?

Jason: Of course not. *(Shepherds draw closer together and sit in silence for a while)*

Nathan: I wonder sometimes if God watches over us, over kids ... like we watch over the sheep.

Jason: I hope so; then we wouldn't have to be scared of ... I mean ...

Thomas: We know what you mean, Jason.

Lydia: Does God love us? Does he really, really love us?

Micah: Yes, I'm sure he does; and yet, sometimes, he seems so far away. Even in the synagogue ... or in the temple ... I mean, I know that he cares for us, but I wish sometimes that he was actually *with us*.

(Suddenly, a bright light comes on above and behind the Shepherds. They grab onto each other as they turn to look in amazement)

Narrator 3: And there were in the same country, shepherds abiding in the field, keeping watch over their flock by night. And, lo, the angel of the Lord came upon them, and the glory of the Lord shone round about them: and they were sore afraid.

Angel: *(Stepping forward)* Fear not: for, behold, I bring you good tidings of great joy, which shall be to all people. For unto you is born this day in the city of David, a Savior, which is Christ the Lord. And this shall be a sign unto you; ye shall find the babe wrapped in swaddling clothes, lying in a manger.

Narrator 4: And suddenly there was with the angel a multitude of the heavenly host praising God, and saying, Glory to God in the highest, and on earth, peace, good will toward men.

Angels, Youth Choir, and/or Congregation sing "Hark! The Herald Angels Sing"

(Light above goes off)

Thomas: Was that an angel?

Titus: Yes, Thomas.

Simon: Angels! I actually saw angels: Wait 'til I tell that know-it-all David!

Jason: I'm going to find Father. *(Runs off, then returns momentarily with great excitement in his voice)* We're going; we're all going into town ... to see a baby ... the ... the Savior ... and his mother and father, too!

Micah: *(As the Shepherds turn to leave)* I'm never going to forget this night.

Nathan: Me neither. You know, somehow God doesn't seem very far away at all ... anymore.

(Lights dim)

Youth Choir sings "Emmanuel" (or other appropriate carol or hymn)

Act 4

(The focus is once again on the manger. Mary and Joseph are awake and gazing down into the manger as the Shepherds approach and the lights come up)

Narrator 3: So they hurried off and found Mary, Joseph, and the baby, who was lying in the manger.

Simon: *(Motioning to the others)* Come on, just one more peek. We couldn't see much with all those *grown-ups* crowding around.

Jason: *(Shouting offstage)* I'll be right there, Dad, as soon as I get Lydia. She's always laggin' behind.

(The Shepherds approach reverently as Mary lifts the baby up into her arms)

Mary: Isn't he beautiful, Joseph? *(Joseph nods)* Can you believe ... angels, a whole company of angels to announce his birth.

Joseph: *(With a smile)* It is right, isn't it, Mary, so very right, that on this night the angels should come? I was getting a little discouraged, with people back home giving us such a hard time ... and the taxes, and the long trip ... and then no room at all for us in the inn ...

Mary: But God has never stopped taking care of us, has he?

Joseph: And he never will. Can you imagine ... he has given to us the joy ... and responsibility ... of bringing up his own Son?

Simon: *(With Lydia at his side)* May we see him? *(Mary nods and leans toward them)* What's his name?

Mary: Jesus.

Lydia: He is beautiful ... but he's so pink!

Nathan: He looks just like any other baby.

Thomas: The angels said that he is the Savior, Christ the Lord ... and our dad says that means that he's also going to be our king.

Titus: *(To Joseph)* Our dad says that you're a carpenter. Will he grow up to be one, too?

Joseph: Yes, I suspect he will.

Micah: Oh, I was hoping that he would be a shepherd like my dad.

Joseph: I'm sure that in his own way, he will.

Jason: Shepherd, carpenter ... *Jesus* ... Savior ... Messiah ... Christ the Lord ... and king!

(Lights dim)

Narrator 4: When they had seen him, they spread the word concerning what had been told about this child, and all who heard it were amazed at what the shepherds said to them. But Mary treasured all these things and pondered them in her heart. The shepherds returned, glorifying and praising God for all the things they had heard and seen.

Children's Choir sings "What Can I Give Him?" (or other appropriate hymn or carol)

Act 5
(As the lights come up, Herod is seen sitting on his throne at the left of the stage, thinking. The stable has once again been transformed into a house and rests in darkness at the right of the stage. The three Wise Men wait at the back of the church and proceed forward slowly as the Narrators speak, whispering and nodding as they come)

Narrator 5: Now when Jesus was born in Bethlehem of Judea in the days of Herod the king, behold, there came Wise Men from the east to Jerusalem, saying, Where is he that is born King of the Jews? For we have seen his star in the east, and are come to worship him.

Narrator 6: When Herod the king had heard these things, he was troubled, and all Jerusalem with him. And when he had gathered all the chief priests and scribes of the people together, he demanded of him where Christ should be born.

Narrator 5: And they said unto him, In Bethlehem of Judea: for thus it is written by the prophet, And thou Bethlehem, in the land of Judea, art not the least among the princes of Judea: for out of thee shall come a governor, that shall rule my people Israel.

Herod: *(Glancing up as the Wise Men approach)* Yes, yes, come on in.

Wise Man 1: *(As they all bow their heads politely)* Your highness, do you have word for us ... of where we should search for the newborn king? And ... and where has everybody gone?

Herod: *(With a wave of his hand)* Oh, them, the priests and the scribes, who needs them...? I do have something to tell you ... in secret. But, first ... a question.

Wise Man 2: *(As they all draw in closer to the Herod)* My lord?

Herod: *(As if discussing a great secret)* Exactly how long ago did you first see this "star" that guides you?

Wise Man 3: Two years ago, King Herod. Why do you ask?

Herod: Ah, never mind, never mind. Now what I have to tell you: There is a place ... a small village called Bethlehem ... five miles south of here ... just off the main road that leads to Hebron ...

Wise Man 1: Yes, I have traveled that road.

Herod: Well, it is in that village that the prophet said the ruler would be born. Now go ... make a careful search for the child ... and as soon as you have found him, report back to me. I'd like to go and worship him, too.

(The Wise Men bow and retreat)

Wise Man 2: *(As they turn to walk away)* Strange man.

(A bright light appears overhead for the Wise Men to follow)

Wise Man 1: *(Looking up)* There, there, my friends ... I see the star! Look, it's moving on ahead of us again. Let's go. Our search is almost done!

(The lights dim on Herod as the Wise Men move toward the back of the church, pausing there, before coming back toward the front again. The Wise Men "search diligently" as they come)

(The lights come up on the manger scene. Mary and Joseph are asleep, the baby either in the manger or in a small bed close to them. The Wise Men approach and stand reverently still, one of them clearing his throat two or three times, each time a bit louder, until he, at last, gets a response)

Joseph: *(Sitting up suddenly)* Mary, what was that?

Mary: *(Sleepily)* What? Hm? I didn't hear anything.

Joseph: *(Standing up and walking forward)* There. There. There are strange men out front ... in strange clothes ... rich clothes ... and with camels behind them!

(Mary instinctively moves closer to the baby)

Joseph: *(Taking another step)* Sirs, who are you ... and why have you come here ... at this hour of the night?

Wise Man 1: We have traveled long and come from far, far away ... to worship ... and to give gifts ... to the newborn king.

Joseph: *(Stepping back in awe)* Come in, please. My home ... our home ... is yours.

(The Wise Men sweep in and then bow, all the way, face-first, to the ground before the child, as Mary and Joseph look on in wonder. Silently then, and reverently, the Wise Men rise up and one-by-one place their gifts before the baby)

(Scene freezes. Lights dim)

Narrator 6: And being warned by God in a dream, that they should not return to Herod, they departed into their own country another way.

Narrator 5: And when they had departed, behold, the angel of the Lord appeared to Joseph in a dream, saying, Arise, and take the young child and his mother, and flee into Egypt, and be thou there until I bring thee word: for Herod will seek the young child to destroy him.

(The lights go out on the stage as the image of the cross appears high up on back wall)

Pastor or Play Director: *(From in front of, or off to the side of, the stage)* And so began the long, hard struggle that was to be Jesus' life. The Son of God came into the world to live among men, to share our joys and fears, triumphs, hardships, and sorrows. And, in the end, to die on the cross, bearing our sins. He was, and is, the Light of the World ... and yet the Bible says that humankind loved the darkness, rather than the light. He came to his own people and yet was thrown out of his own synagogue in his own hometown. "He was in the world, and the world was made by him," as John's Gospel says, "and the world knew him not." And yet for those of us who, through the ages, have come to know him personally ... he is Jesus ... Emmanuel, God with us ... Son of God ... King Eternal ... the Great Shepherd ... the Lamb of God ... the Light of Life ... the Savior of the world. It is our prayer that tonight, if he is not already, he would become your Savior, too.

Director's Notes

Director's Notes

Time Travelers' Tales Of The Carols

A One-Act Play
With Carol Singing

Linda Buff
and
Sharon Cathcart

Time Travelers' Tales Of The Carols

Characters

Lisa (a teenager)
Rachel (Lisa's friend)
Jeff (Lisa's younger brother)
Tina
Zach
Ryan
Kevin
Haley
Beth
Laura
Jacob
Youngest Child

Charles Wesley (at age 32)
John Henry Hopkins, Jr. (at age 37)
Phillips Brooks (at age 34)
Father Mohr (at age 26)
Franz Gruber (at age 31)
Henry Wadsworth Longfellow (at age 56)
Pastor Brad (present-day church leader)
Mary (non-speaking)
Joseph (non-speaking)
Angel
Shepherds (non-speaking)

Costumes

Lisa wears a lab coat. Each of the "time travelers" are dressed in costumes reflecting the era of their time; some use props. Children are dressed in modern-day clothing. Additional Wise Men costumes are needed, which will be put on the children as "dress-up" clothing.

Setting

The basement of Lisa and Jeff's house, which Lisa uses as her "lab." Upstage center is the "time machine" which Lisa and Rachel have built.

Props

The time machine may be constructed from a refrigerator box, and made to look modernistic with lots of aluminum foil, dials on front, and flashing lights. Its front is covered with a curtain. It has a false back to allow the men to go in and out from behind. Use a synthesizer to make noises when the time machine is operated. CDs are needed, containing the hymns to be used. A karaoke machine sits downstage center. A low desk, containing a laptop computer, pen and paper, a Bible, and a telephone, is downstage right. Basement walls are decorated with posters that reflect Lisa's interests, such as Albert Einstein, a periodic table of the elements, and Christian themes. A chair and guitar stand with guitar are upstage. A nativity tableau will take place downstage left, where there is a manger, a baby, and perhaps a few other stable props.

(Lisa and Rachel are in the lab. Jeff, holding several CD cases, is knocking on the door to the lab. His two friends, Tina and Zach, are with him)

Jeff: Lisa! Are you in here? I need your help!

Lisa: *(Opens door and looks out with some suspicion)* Okay ... what do you need?

Jeff: I need help with a report. We have a Sunday school assignment to research a Christmas carol. I'm supposed to be able to tell all about "Hark! The Herald Angels Sing."

Lisa: Great! What have you got so far?

Jeff: A bunch of CDs with Christmas carols.

Rachel: Is that all?

Jeff: Well, you're so smart I thought you could help me ... pleeeease? Hey, what's that behind you? *(Pushes Lisa aside excitedly)*

Lisa: It's a time machine. We've been working on it for months.

Tina: Way cool! Does it work?

Rachel: We're not sure. Maybe we could try it out for your research project?

Lisa: Who wrote "Hark! The Herald Angels Sing"?

Jeff: *(Fumbling with several CDs)* Oh, here. Charles Wesley.

Lisa: *(Punches buttons on the laptop)* Charles Wesley. Preacher and cofounder of Methodism. He wrote over 6,000 hymns.

Jeff: *(Looking over Lisa's shoulder)* Looks like he wrote "Hark! The Herald Angels Sing" in 1739 in England.

Lisa: Okay, here goes.

(Lisa turns dials on machine and punches buttons. Space-age noises emanate from machine. Lisa pulls back curtain of time machine to reveal a man formally dressed in 1700s-era clothing, standing there looking startled)

Jeff, Lisa, Rachel, Tina, Zach: *Whoa!* It works!

Wesley: What has happened? Who are you? And why are you all dressed so strangely?

Rachel: You've traveled in time to the year 2004.

Lisa: If you can help us a bit, we will send you back soon. *(Stage-whispers to others)* I hope it works in reverse!

Jeff: Reverend Wesley! I understand that you wrote the words to a Christmas song in the 1730s. Do you remember that?

Wesley: Oh, most assuredly! What a remarkable moment that was. *(Looking lost in thought)*

Jeff: *(Grabs pen and paper to make notes)* Could you tell us about it?

Wesley: It was a lovely Christmas Day in London. I was walking to church. The joyous sounds of the church bells resounded all around me, stirring my soul and filling me with a sense of the magnificence of the occasion of Jesus' birth. I was prodigiously inspired, and I wrote down the verses which I titled *(Grandly)* "Hark, How All The Welkin Rings" ...

Jeff: *(Stops writing, puzzled)* You wrote *what*?

Wesley: "Hark, How All The Welkin Rings."

Jeff: Oh, I get it. Is *welkin* another word for angels?

Wesley: Of course not, my dear lad. Welkin — it refers to — all the heavens. "Hark, How All The Heavens Ring."

Rachel: But, sir, we know the song now as "Hark, The Herald Angels Sing."

Jeff: Yeah, let me pop the CD into the karaoke machine and play it for you.

Wesley: *(Pauses)* I thought you were speaking English until that last sentence.

(Youth sing "Hark! The Herald Angels Sing" with karaoke machine)

Lisa: Even now in the year 2004, it's one of the favorite Christmas carols, sir.

Jeff: Yeah, one of the best in the whole welkin!

Wesley: Thanks be to God. I never dreamed it would be that enduring. Now, my young friends, if you could be so kind as to send me back to the eighteenth century. *(Gets back into time machine)* Godspeed!

(They close the curtain; Lisa sets dials. Machine beeps and noises. They open the curtain and he is gone. They look pleased)

Jeff: I'm going to go call Laura and tell her what we're doing! *(Uses phone)*

(Ryan, Kevin, and Haley enter)

Ryan: Jeff, can you come out and ride scooters with us? Hey, what are you guys doing?

Tina: We're working on research projects about Christmas carols.

Haley: Yay! Christmas is only one week away!

Kevin: I love Christmas! I love hearing about how Frosty the Snowman was born in a manger.

Ryan: And the shepherds looked up in the sky and saw Santa Claus in his sleigh full of toys!

Haley: And how Rudolph, with his nose so bright, guided the three Wise Men to the stable.

(Lisa, Rachel, Tina, and Zach look at each other)

Rachel: Uh, you've got things a little mixed up there. Christmas is the time when Jesus was born. He's the Son of God.

Zach: Mary, Jesus' mother, and her husband Joseph, traveled to Bethlehem, but it was so crowded that they had to stay in a stable.

Tina: *(Opening the Bible to Luke 2. As she reads, Joseph and Mary enter stage right, cross to downstage left, place baby in manger, and kneel next to him)* "He went there to register with Mary, who was pledged to be married to him and was expecting a child. While they were there, the time came for the baby to be born, and she gave birth to her firstborn, a son. She wrapped him in cloths and placed him in a manger, because there was no room for them in the inn."

Zach: *(As Zach reads, Shepherds enter and stand center stage. Angel enters and faces them. They kneel)* "And there were shepherds living out in the fields nearby, keeping watch over their flocks at night. An angel of the Lord appeared to them, and they were terrified. But the angel said to them,

Angel: 'Do not be afraid. I bring you good news of great joy that will be for all the people. Today in the town of David, a Savior has been born to you; he is Christ the Lord. This will be a sign to you: You will find a baby wrapped in cloths and lying in a manger.' "

(Shepherds go to manger and kneel by it, Angel exits)

Rachel: Frosty and Santa and Rudolph are fun, but Christmas is really about Jesus.

Tina: Lisa, can you help me with my report? I'm confused about my Christmas carol, "We Three Kings of Orient Are." It doesn't make any sense.

Haley: I know. I've never been able to figure out where Orient-Are is.

Zach: Haley, they're just saying it fancy. It means the kings are from the Orient, which we now call Asia.

Haley: Oh. Well, then, what are you so confused about, Tina?

Tina: Well, it doesn't say anywhere in the Bible that the Wise Men were kings. And it doesn't say there were three of them. And it doesn't say they were from the Orient.

Zach: Let's bring the person here who wrote the song and ask him!

Lisa: Okay. Who is it, Tina? What year, and where did he live?

Tina: His name was John Henry Hopkins, Jr. He wrote the words and music in 1857 in New York City.

(Lisa sets and turns dials. Everyone hovers around excitedly. Open curtains and Hopkins, dressed 1800s-era, appears)

Tina: Are you the Reverend John Henry Hopkins?

Hopkins: Indeed I am. And who, may I ask, are you? And why are all of you dressed so strangely?

Tina: A time machine brought you to the year 2004. And we are fans of the Christmas song you wrote about the three kings.

Hopkins: *(Smiles broadly)* That song is still known in the year 2004? I would never have dreamed it.

Tina: But, sir, the Bible doesn't say that the Wise Men were kings, or how many there were, or where they were from.

Hopkins: Good for you, young lady! You've been reading your Bible! And you are right. The Bible says that three very expensive gifts were brought to Jesus. Gold is a precious metal, frankincense was a special gum resin from trees used to burn as incense, and myrrh was also a gum resin used to make incense and perfume. Since there were three gifts, it is logical to assume that there were three men. And since they presented such fine and expensive gifts, it is logical to assume they were of very high station, such as kings. Many people think they were also astronomers who studied the skies and knew that the star announced something very special.

Kevin: And the part about the Orient?

Hopkins: Matthew 2:1 says that they came from the east, so they might have come from Persia or some other Oriental country. At any rate, it makes a good story, don't you think?

Haley: Oh, yes! It's my favorite!

Hopkins: *(Smiles and squats to Haley's level)* Why, you remind me of my little niece. She loved my song, too. Did you know that I wrote it as a Christmas present for my nieces and nephews?

All: You did, really?

Hopkins: Every Christmas I travel to Vermont to be with my relatives. My nieces and nephews always expect something special from their old Uncle Henry, and I couldn't disappoint them! So one year, I wrote this song for them. I taught it to them and they acted it out for the rest of the family! What a wonderful holiday that was!

(Tina puts CD into karaoke machine and plays "We Three Kings." Children dress up Ryan, Kevin, and Haley as kings. As the others sing the song, they go to the manger and place gifts at Mary's feet)

Hopkins: We had such a jolly time together that Christmas, I don't know what kind of present I can ever take to the children to match it.

Ryan: How about a Nintendo?

Haley: Or the new Barbie video!

Hopkins: *(Pauses)* I have no idea what you are talking about. I think I should return to the comforts of the nineteenth century now.

Lisa: Sure. *(Whispers to youth)* I hope this is still working.

(Everyone waves good-bye; they close curtain. Buttons, dials, noises, open curtain and he is gone)

(The door opens and Beth, Laura, and Jacob enter)

Laura: Hey, what's going on? Are you really bringing people here from the past to help you write your Sunday school reports?

All: Yes!

Laura: Wow! That's better than the Internet!

Beth: Can you bring me the man who wrote "O Little Town Of Bethlehem"?

Rachel: No problem. Give us his name, the year of the song, and what place.

Beth: The name is Phillip Brooks, 1868. *(Shrugs)* I guess he must have lived in Bethlehem.

Lisa: I believe you mean *Phillips* Brooks. He was a well-known Episcopalian minister in Boston.

Beth: Phillips? That's a funny name.

Kevin: Did he invent the screwdriver, too?

All: I don't think so.

(Lisa pushes buttons and dials; machine emits noises. Beth opens curtain to reveal Brooks, wearing dark clothes and clerical collar)

Beth: Welcome, Reverend Brooks.

Brooks: Oh, my, where am I? And why are all of you dressed so strangely?

Beth: We brought you to the year 2004 in a time machine. Are you the one who wrote the song "O Little Town of Bethlehem"?

Brooks: Yes, young lady, I authored the words to the song. I didn't know it would be so enduring.

Beth: Well, did you live in Bethlehem?

Brooks: No, but I did have the great privilege of traveling through that Holy Land one year. *(Jeff brings chair, Brooks sits down, and children gather around him)* In fact, on the day before Christmas in the year 1865, I was riding a horse from Jerusalem to Bethlehem. My companions and I looked around Bethlehem, then rode out to the fields near there. That's where the shepherds were on the night Jesus was born! Somewhere in those fields we rode through, an angel appeared to the shepherds. As we rode past, there were still shepherds "keeping watch over their flocks!"

All: Wow! Really?

Brooks: Then I went and joined in the worship service in the Church of the Nativity. That is the church build right over the cave where they say that Jesus was born! That service started at 10:00 and ended at 3:00 in the morning! *(Children react)* That is a night I shall remember to the end of my days.

Beth: Is that when you wrote the song?

Brooks: No, my dear, it was not until three years subsequent, back in my own church in Philadelphia. In our church, every year at Christmas, we have a special program, and the Sunday school children sing songs ...

Zach: Yeah, in our church, too!

Brooks: Recalling how inspired I was to look out over the shepherds' fields and gaze into the town of Bethlehem, I penned some verses, "How silently, how silently the wondrous gift is given! So God imparts to human hearts the blessings of His heaven." *(Gazes afar as if to relive those moments)*

Beth: So the children sang the song in the program?

Brooks: Yes, but it almost didn't happen!

Beth: Why not?

Brooks: I asked my friend, Lewis Redner, who is our church organist, to write the music for it. Alas! It came to be the very day before Christmas and Lewis had not been able to compose a suitable tune. I began to despair ... I suppose we adults can become a bit overwrought about the annual Christmas program ...

Zach: Yeah, in our church, too!

(Everyone agrees)

Brooks: But that very night, a most miraculous event occurred. Lewis awakened in the night with what he called "an angel strain" playing in his mind. He quickly wrote down the melody. Lewis calls it "a gift from heaven." The next day, the children sang the song in the program.

(Youth sing "O Little Town Of Bethlehem" with karaoke machine)

Beth: The music came as a gift from heaven, just as Jesus came to us as a gift from heaven.

Brooks: Precisely! And with that, dear children, could you please send me back to my own time, as I am quite busy readying for Christmas?

Lisa: No problem. Thanks for coming.

(Lisa sends him back in same manner as before)

Tina: This machine is awesome. Lisa, you're so smart!

Jeff: Yeah, she's the smartest sister in all the welkin!

All: All the what?

Jeff: Welkin — it means "heavens." Don't you guys know anything?

Beth: Jacob, what Christmas carol are you researching?

Jacob: "Silent Night." But I already know about how it was written. There was this church in Austria, you know, like in the *Sound of Music*? And a little church mouse chewed a hole in the organ bellows, so the organ didn't work. But, it was Christmas, and they wanted to have some music for the Christmas service, so the priest wrote the song "Silent Night."

Laura: Is that true?

Jacob: Well, I'm not really sure. That's what my mom heard somewhere.

Ryan: Let's bring the priest here and ask him!

Jacob: Okay. It was the year 1818 in Austria.

(Lisa operates machine and when they open curtain, Mohr and Gruber step out)

Rachel: Oops. We got two people.

Mohr and Gruber: *(Together, in German accent)* Who are you? And why are you dressed so strangely?

Jacob: You've been brought to the year 2004. Is either of you Father Mohr, who wrote the song "Silent Night"?

Mohr: *Ya*, I am the man who wrote the words to *"Stille Nacht."* And you have also gotten the man who composed the music — this is the organist of my church, Franz Gruber.

Jacob: Did you really write the song because a mouse ruined your organ?

Mohr: *(He and Gruber look at each other with puzzled looks)* A mouse...? *Acht, nein.* It was no little church mouse that did it. You see, our organ had gotten very rusty ...

Gruber: The river Salzach flows very close to our church, and the air is very damp. It is not *goot* for a pipe organ.

Mohr: Although it is a very beautiful river, flowing through our village in the Alps ...

Gruber: *Ya*, but the damp air is not *goot* for the organ, Father.

Mohr: That is true, Franz. *Chust* before Christmas, I find that the organ does not work ...

Gruber: It was the rust.

Mohr: ... but we must have music for the Christmas Eve Mass! So I wrote down words for a song: *"Stille nacht, heilige nacht...."* And I took them to Herr Gruber ...

Gruber: When I read them, I say, "Friend Mohr, you have found it — the right song — God be praised!" It was the most perfect Christmas hymn I had ever seen.

Mohr: And Herr Gruber wrote music just as perfect. We sang the new hymn at the Christmas Mass.

Jacob: But you still didn't have an organ!

Mohr: *Ya*, so Herr Gruber played his guitar.

(Jeff takes guitar from stand upstage and hands it to Gruber. Youth sing "Silent Night" as Gruber accompanies on guitar)

Gruber: Father, tell them what happened after that, about Herr Karl.

Mohr: *Ya.* A few days later, an organ builder came to repair the organ. He liked the song, and took a copy of it with him. He spread it all around Tyrol, and it became very popular as a folk song.

Gruber: Now people sing it all over Austria.

Jacob: Even more than that. People sing it all over the world!

Mohr: *(To Gruber)* Did you think the song would endure for so long?

Gruber: *Nein.* God be praised.

Jacob: Thank you for sharing your story and your beautiful song with us.

Mohr: If you could be so kind as to ... send us back to our proper place in time...?

(As Mohr and Gruber enter the time machine, children call out "Good-bye;" men say, "Auf wiedersein." Lisa sends them back as before)

Kevin: What song are you researching, Laura?

Laura: "I Heard The Bells On Christmas Day."

Rachel: Well, tell us who wrote it and when.

Laura: Henry Wadsworth Longfellow in 1863.

(Lisa operates machine and Laura pulls back the curtain. Longfellow is dressed in Civil War-era clothing)

Longfellow: Who are you? And why are you all dressed so strangely?

Laura: You're in the year 2004. Can you tell us what made you write the song "I Heard The Bells On Christmas Day"?

Longfellow: *(Long, thoughtful sigh)* I did not know that song would last so long. At any rate, I wrote it during the vicious and bloody Civil War. The North and the South were fighting and I thought the United States would be torn apart. I was very distraught. It seemed as if evil was winning over good. It seemed as if there would be no peace. As I awoke, I thought that the true message of Christmas would be drowned out by war.

Laura: Then you heard the bells?

Longfellow: Oh, yes. Church bells began to ring and echo across the land. The message of Christmas was loud and clear as the bells announced: "Peace on Earth, Good will toward Man."

(Youth sing "I Heard The Bells On Christmas Day" with karaoke machine)

Laura: That's a message that we need to hear today, also, Mr. Longfellow. Thank you for coming and reminding us.

(Lisa sends Longfellow back as before)

Beth: We've learned so much! Let's call Pastor Brad and tell him what we've done.

Tina: Let's bring him here in the time machine!

Lisa: I can bring people from the past, but I don't know how to transport someone here from the present.

Zach: Well, then, just bring him here from, like, 6:00 this morning.

Lisa: Okay.

(Lisa operates time machine in usual manner, bringing Pastor Brad, unshaven, with rumpled hair, wearing bathrobe, and holding cup of coffee)

All: Good morning, Pastor Brad!

Pastor Brad: *(Not quite awake, puzzled, overwhelmed by youth all around him)* Where am I?

All: And why are *you* dressed so strangely?

Beth: You're in Lisa's basement.

Zach: We've been working on our Christmas carol reports and have great things to tell you!

Pastor Brad: *(Sits down; youth gather around)* Tell me about it.

Haley: Music sure is a big part of celebrating Christmas.

Jeff: Especially if the music is *enduring*.

Pastor Brad: What elements are in the most enduring carols?

Beth: The manger.

Laura: Shepherds.

Youngest Child: Jesus!

Jacob: The star.

Ryan: Mary and Joseph.

Youngest Child: Jesus!

Haley: Peace.

Tina: The Wise Men.

Youngest Child: Jesus!

Kevin: "The First Noel" has all those elements.

Zach: I like "Joy To The World."

Pastor Brad: Let's all sing those carols.

(Congregation joins youth in singing "The First Noel" and "Joy To The World")

Tina: Christmas carols are enduring because they remind us how much God loves us, and that's why he sent his only Son to earth.

Zach: And when we know Jesus as Savior and Lord, that's the best Christmas gift in the whole world!

Haley: The best gift in all the welkin!

All: Merry Christmas!

Youngest Child: Happy birthday, Jesus!

Bibliography

Collins, Ace. *Stories Behind the Best-Loved Songs of Christmas.* Grand Rapids: Zondervan, 2001.

Colquhoun, Frank. *Hymns That Live.* Downers Grove, Illinois: InterVarsity Press, 1980.

Osbeck, Kenneth W. *Singing With Understanding.* Grand Rapids: Kregel Publications, 1979.

Studwell, William. *The Christmas Carol Reader.* New York: Harrington Park Press, 1995.

Director's Notes

Director's Notes

Here We Come To Bethlehem

A Christmas Pageant
For The Whole Congregation

Pamela Honan Peterson

Here We Come To Bethlehem

Characters

Narrator

Leah and Joel — two onlookers (If necessary, both can be girls or boys. Change Joel to Anna or change Leah to David, whichever is needed)

Response Speaker(s) (may be read by one speaker or as many as six)

Mary

Joseph

Donkey

Weary Travelers (two or more; any age combination)

Child Travelers (just old enough to read or learn lines)

Shepherds (two or more)

Sheep (age 3-5, any number)

Angel(s) (at least one)

Wise Men (two or more)

Running Time

20 to 25 minutes

Synopsis

The audience eavesdrops as ancient travelers make their way to Bethlehem and listens to their thoughts, stories, and questions. Little do they know that God, the Lord of all, has the biggest story to tell, and that it is for every traveler on the road, including us. And God's story — God's actions — will answer all the questions, right here in Bethlehem.

Costumes

Biblical costumes can be as basic or as elaborate as desired. The Narrator is outside the action of the story, so should wear contemporary clothing. Because the Donkey provides some humor in the script, it can be fun to provide a costume that adds to the humor. For example, try making an oversized head from a brown bag, with stuffed brown-bag ears attached; or consider renting a costume. Wise Men should carry objects decorated to look like gifts — perhaps boxes covered with bright foil or fabric.

Stage Setting and Props

Any open area such as a stage or church chancel may be used. The setting is a stable scene. This can be as simple as a manger containing a doll, or it may be more elaborate, using props to indicate the surrounding stable building. A path or road should be indicated from the back of the room to the stable scene. It may go along a center aisle or along one side, angling toward the stable. It may be as simple as lengths of cardboard laid end to end with stone outlines drawn on them. Seating should be provided for the cast at the back of the room (or just outside the room but within easy earshot) where performers can wait to walk along the "road" to the stable when their turn comes. Depending on the size of the cast, several adults should be with the group to monitor noise and to send characters forward at the appointed times. A lectern or music stand should be placed just to one side of the set for the Narrator, Joel and Leah, and Response Speakers.

Music and Sound

Hymns and songs are suggested, but others with similar themes may be used in place of any of them. It may help to have a standing microphone to one side of the set for Narrator, Joel, Leah, and Response Speakers to use, and a hand mike for other speaking characters.

Production Notes

This program is written for about eighteen performers, ranging from age three through high school. It can expand to as many children and youth as you have, who want to be involved. If needed or desired, adults can fill some roles, for example, Shepherds, Wise Men, and Travelers. Any number of very young children can be Sheep, Angels, and part of the group of Weary Travelers. Performers with speaking parts may present them as readings or memorize them. Most are short monologues.

Here We Come To Bethlehem

Brief Welcome by Pastor or Other Leader

Congregation sings "O Little Town Of Bethlehem," verse 1.

Invocation/Prayer (*May be done with congregation reading and children saying responses, or with an individual reading and congregation — or children — saying responses*)

Reading:	Jesus, you love us and you came to be one of us.
Response:	**Thank you. Thank you.**
Reading:	You were born in a village, born to be with us.
Response:	**Thank you. Thank you.**
Reading:	You were a real baby, born in a stable.
Response:	**Thank you. Thank you.**
Reading:	You came to save us from sin and sadness.
Response:	**Thank you. Thank you.**
Reading:	You came to give us new life!
Response:	**Thank you. Thank you.**
All:	**Guide us now and help us see** **Just how all this came to be. Amen.**

(Joel and Leah move to lectern and speak or read with much expression)

Joel: Wow! Look at the crowds! This is a noisy time to live in Bethlehem! I wonder how many people are coming here to be counted in this census.

Leah: Why does everyone have to be counted, anyway?

Joel: So the emperor will know how many people there are so he can make each one pay taxes — money to build more palaces for him, and *maybe* a road or two for the rest of us.

Leah: It is hard to believe all these people are *here.* I mean, nothing ever happens in little ol' Bethlehem. The last exciting thing I remember was the time some of old Jacob's sheep wandered away from the flock and came into town and tried to eat some of the green stuff out of Uncle Saul's vegetable stall.

Joel: Yeah. Including some leeks. Phew! A sheep with onion breath!

Leah: Well — maybe with so many people in town, something more interesting than that will happen. Let's look around.

Joel: Look over there where that lady is on that donkey, with the man walking beside her. The lady is going to have a baby. She looks really tired. And the man looks kind of worried.

Leah: Let's get a little closer and see if we can hear what they're saying.

Why Are We Going To Bethlehem? — Mary
(Narrator joins Joel and Leah)

Narrator: As travelers make their way to Bethlehem, they have their own thoughts, their own stories, and above all, their own questions. Little do they know that God the Lord of all has the biggest story to tell, and that it is for every traveler on the road, including us. And God's story — God's actions — will answer all the questions, right here in Bethlehem.
Listen to God's promise through the prophet Micah about this little town.

Narrator reads Micah 5:2.

(Mary moves along "road" to stable, speaks, and takes her place behind the manger. Response Speaker 1 moves to mike)

Mary: Why are we going to Bethlehem? It's a hard journey, and a far-away place. Why must my baby be born there, so far from my home and my family? Why are we going to Bethlehem?

Response Speaker 1: Bethlehem is the city of David. God promised that someone would come one day from David's town to save God's people. David was a shepherd. He cared for his sheep. He saved them from danger. He was also a king.
Your Son will be our true Shepherd, the Shepherd of our hearts. He will save us from sin and death. He is the King of the Universe, and will reign in our hearts.
In Bethlehem, God will be born as a baby, becoming like us so we may truly become like God.

Mary: "I am the Lord's servant. May it be to me as you have said" (Luke 1:38a).

Congregation sings "Once In Royal David's City," verses 1 and 2.

How Far Will It Be To Bethlehem? — Joseph

Joel: The man traveling with the lady looks at the lady a lot.

Leah: Yeah, I wonder what he's thinking?

(Joseph moves along "road" to stable, speaks, then goes to stand beside Mary. Response Speaker 2 moves to mike)

Joseph: How far will it be to Bethlehem? The road *is* so long, up hill and down. It's rocky and crowded, and Mary is tired. She needs to rest. The baby is coming, and it's not just *any* baby. How far will it be to Bethlehem?

Response Speaker 2: Yes, Joseph, the road is long. But God is with you and Mary your beloved — and most surely with the baby. This is the right road. It leads to the place where the Son of God will be born, just as the prophets said. What better path could there be?

Narrator reads Luke 2:1, 4-6.

Congregation or group of children sings to the tune of "Twinkle, Twinkle, Little Star."
Joseph, Joseph, kind and true,
Strong and caring, God loves you,
Gave you special work to do —
Loving Mary, Jesus, too.
Joseph, Joseph, God loves you,
Gave you special work to do.

What Will I Hear In Bethlehem? — Donkey

Joel: Look at that donkey Mary is riding on! It sure has big ears. And donkeys sound funny, too.

Leah: Yeah. But, he almost looks kind of worried right now. I wonder what he's thinking.

(Donkey moves along "road" to stable, speaks with exaggerated expression and movements, and stands a little way apart from people. Response Speaker 3 moves to mike)

Donkey: What will I hear in Bethlehem? I am glad to carry the tired lady, but I'm only a little donkey. Will I hear people laughing at my small size, my big ears, my loud braying, my stubborn personality — which is my *only defense* against all that laughing, you know? Will I be bombarded by the boisterous bellowing of humans running everywhere, arguing and selling, and calling children? What will I hear?

Response Speaker 3: Little creature, you will hear all of this. But you'll also hear doves cooing, sheep bleating, and cows mooing — all at peace and waiting for the baby. And you'll hear the lady saying, "Thank you," for carrying her, tired and cold and needing your soft back for rest. Of course you'll hear a baby crying. And when you do, it will be *God* coming to bring redemption and peace to *all* creation — including you, little creature.

76

Narrator reads Romans 8:19a; Isaiah 11:6-9.

Congregation sings "The Friendly Beasts," verse 1.
I, said the donkey, shaggy and brown,
I carried his mother up hill and down,
I carried her safely to Bethlehem town;
I, said the donkey all shaggy and brown.
                    — Twelfth-century carol

What Will We Understand In Bethlehem? — Weary Travelers
Joel: Boy! Those people there look exhausted, especially the children.

Leah: Yeah. I'm glad we already live here. I wouldn't want to have to walk for days.

(Weary Travelers move along "road" to stable, one speaks, then all go to stand in the stable area. Response Speaker 4 moves to mike)

Weary Traveler: What will we understand in Bethlehem? We're only weary travelers, coming to do our duty to Caesar — to be counted so that we can be taxed. We are cold and hungry. We just want to be at home with our families, warm and comfortable again.

Yet, as we come nearer to the city, we feel expectation in the air! Is our journey *more* than a duty to be done? What *will* we understand in Bethlehem?

Response Speaker 4: You will begin to understand a wonderful mystery. A baby born in Bethlehem tonight will be God in the flesh! Can you imagine? The air will be alive with angels and stars. God comes to shower love and hope and freedom on all people — especially on you who are so weary and in need. Some day, this child will say:

Narrator reads Luke 6:20b-21.

Congregation sings "It Came Upon The Midnight Clear," verse 3.

What Will I Do In Bethlehem? — Child Traveler
(Child Traveler moves along "road" to stable, speaks, then joins group of Weary Travelers in scene. Response Speaker 5 moves to mike)

Child Traveler: What will I do in Bethlehem? I am a little child. Will I have fun and run? Can I dance and sing? What will I *do* in Bethlehem?

Response Speaker 5: Oh, yes, you will be *very joyful* in Bethlehem — for a child will be born there tonight. He will be your older brother who comes to love you and protect you and show you the way to happiness! You can dance and sing. You can run like the wind in circles of smiles.

Combined or Individual Children's or Youths' Voices or Narrator reads Psalm 149:1-3.

Congregation sings "I Danced In The Morning," verse 1.

What Will We See In Bethlehem? — Shepherds, Sheep, Angels

(Shepherds, Sheep, and one or more Angels move along "road" to stable and all move into scene. Response Speaker 6 moves to mike)

Joel: Whoa! Here come some shepherds — and sheep! It's a good thing Uncle Saul's food stall is closed. Hey — what's the matter? You look like you've seen a ghost.

Leah: N-no. I think I see *an angel (or angels)* with the shepherds. Something amazing is happening!

Narrator reads Luke 2:8-12, 15.

Shepherd: What will we see in Bethlehem? We are only shepherds, but we have already seen angels tonight! We can't imagine anything more amazing than that. But, the angels said we must come and see a baby in a stable who would bring God's love and peace to the whole wide world. They said he would be the Savior and bring joy to all people. Surely, that is even better than angels! What will we see in Bethlehem?

Response Speaker 6: You will see just what the angels promised to you! The baby is the Savior who will save the world from the darkness of sin and death and give us life forever with God. Could there be a more amazing sight than this? Bring along your lambs so they also may see the Lamb of God. Then go and spread the good news!

Congregation sings "Go, Tell It On The Mountain," verses 1 and 2.

What Shall We Bring To Bethlehem? — Wise Men
Narrator reads Matthew 2:1b-2, 9b-12.

Joel: This must be a special baby! Here come some men who look really rich and from somewhere really far from here.

Leah: They've got presents, and they're walking up to the stable as if it were a palace. Let's join them.

(Wise Men move along "road" to stable. One speaks, Joel and Leah move to a spot closer to those in the scene, though off just a bit to the side)

Wise Man: What shall we bring to Bethlehem? We are Wise Men who have come in search of a great new king. A bright star has led us here, and we come to honor him. But what can we give him if he is truly the ruler of all that is? No gift is fine enough for that! What shall we bring to Bethlehem?

Older Children and Youth Voices, or Narrator speaks.
Bring myrrh and bring incense, most fragrant and rare
To anoint him God's holy one, loving and fair.

Bring gold to the baby to show he is king.
Bring worship and praises. Bring everything!

Bring greatest rejoicing for God's loving grace.
Bring voices to shout God's good news every place!

For all future ages must know God is here.
You can tell first what all nations must hear!

(All players look at baby in manger, or Mary may carefully walk through the group, letting each see the baby up close)

Children sing "Away In A Manger," verse 1.

(All remain on stage for prayer and final hymn)

Narrator: On that ancient night, the little town of Bethlehem became great because God arrived there as a human child to be earth's one true hope. He *has become* our peace, and we are glad!

Closing by Pastor or Other Leader: Dear loving God, thank you that Jesus came to be born in Bethlehem as a real baby. Thank you for taking care of him there, and for sending him to save us from sin and to give us new life, now and forever. Let us spread the good news! Amen.

Congregation sings "As With Gladness Men Of Old," verse 1, adapted.
As with gladness men of old
Did the guiding star behold;
As with joy they hailed its light,
Leading onward, beaming bright,
So, most precious God may we
Share your love with all we see.
　　　　　— William Chatterton Dix (Last line, P.H.P.)

Director's Notes

Director's Notes

Choices

A Christmas Service And Pageant
For The Whole Congregation

J. B. Quisenberry

Revised. Originally published in 1990 as *Choices*, copyright 1990, by CSS Publishing Company, Lima, Ohio (1-55673-248-9).

Choices

Characters

Oldest Child
Father
Younger Child
Mother
Leader
Reader (eight)
Wealthy Woman
Innkeeper
Merchant
Joseph (non-speaking)
Mary (non-speaking)
Innkeeper's Wife (non-speaking)
Shepherds (non-speaking)
Angels (non-speaking)

Running Time

50 minutes (approx.)

Costumes

Costumes can range from bathrobes to authentic period clothing.

Setting

The setting for the Opening Skit is a modern living room with a small table to the right. The setting for the Pageant is a stable scene with a manger.

Production Notes

This service is designed to involve a large number of children from the age of three years through high school. Very young children may be used as both Shepherds and Angels, as long as there are older Angels and Shepherds to guide them. Mary, Joseph, Innkeeper and Innkeeper's Wife are best played by fifth or sixth graders. Readers and the other characters should come from the junior high and high school classes. They may present their parts either as dramatic readings or memorized monologues, with or without special costumes. The beginning skit should be done by two fifth, sixth, or seventh graders as Oldest Child and Younger Child and two high school students as Mother and Father. Leader may be either an adult or a high school student.

Prelude

Opening Skit

(Father is working at a small table to the right and Oldest Child and Younger Child are playing on the floor, center stage. The choir, wearing hats and scarves to suggest outerwear, enters singing a traditional Christmas hymn. They proceed toward the left side of the altar area. A doorbell rings, and Oldest Child crosses down left and pantomimes opening a door)

Oldest Child: Look! Christmas carolers! *(Younger Child runs to door)* Dad, come quick! There are carolers at the door!

Father: That's nice. *(Doesn't look up from his work)*

Younger Child: Dad, hurry up! You'll miss them!

Father: I don't have time right now. I've got to finish this report. You can tell me about it later.

Younger Child: *(Runs right and calls offstage)* Mom! There are carolers outside! Come and see them!

Mother: *(From offstage)* I'll be there in a minute, Honey. I've got to get these cookies into the oven or you won't have any for your party at school tomorrow.

(Choir stops singing and exits to the choir loft. Children pantomime closing door and go back to their places on the floor)

Mother: *(Enters from right)* The cookies are all ready for tomorrow. I thought you said that there were carolers at the door.

Oldest Child: We did.

Younger Child: They were great!

Oldest Child: It was really neat! You missed it, Mom.

(Lights out, spotlight on choir. During the black out, the set should be changed to a stable setting)

Welcome

Leader: Welcome to you, and peace to you all! We come together today in celebration of and remembrance of that most blessed night so many years ago, when the stillness of the winter sky was pierced by a baby's first cry. In what better way can we remember that night than through the actions of our own children? As the prophet said, "A little child shall lead them." Come with us now to that holy night when the miracle of birth was visited upon a young couple from Nazareth and the miracle of salvation came to all people in the form of a tiny baby. Come and wonder with the shepherds at that most wonderful event — the birth of Christ!

Choral Anthem   "O Come, O Come, Emmanuel"
(During the anthem, choir members will read the following verses from Isaiah, one after each of the first, second, and third verses of the song)

1. Isaiah 7:14. *Therefore the Lord himself shall give you a sign; Behold a virgin shall conceive, and bear a son, and shall call his name Immanuel.*

2. Isaiah 9:2. *The people that walked in darkness have seen a great light; they that dwell in the land of the shadow of death, upon them hath the light shined.*

3. Isaiah 9:6. *For unto us a child is born, unto us a son is given: and the government shall be upon his shoulder: and his name shall be called Wonderful, Counsellor, The Mighty God, The Everlasting Father, The Prince of Peace.*

The Pageant

(Lights come up on the manger)

Reader 1: When Caesar Augustus made his tax decree, it was a hardship for many. The roads were filled with people going to be counted and taxed in the cities of their ancestors.

Among this throng, there was a couple from Nazareth. There was nothing unusual about them, just a carpenter and his wife, expecting their first child. Thousands must have passed them on the road to Bethlehem without a second glance. And yet, the baby that would be born to this couple would change the world forever.

Wealthy Woman: There were so many people on the road that day! All of us were in a hurry. You see, it was obvious to everyone that it would be difficult to find a place to stay in the City of David. Bethlehem didn't have nearly enough inns to accommodate so many people.

Of course, I wasn't as worried as some. I was sure to get there ahead of the crowd. My team of horses would see to that. I could travel much faster than most of the people, who were on foot. Besides, I was sure to find a room, even if I arrived in the city of my ancestors late. Money speaks loudly, you see. I knew that many of my fellow travelers would not be so fortunate.

I almost stopped and offered one couple a ride. They looked so tired, and the young woman was great with child. But you have to be careful, you know. You can never tell about strangers, no matter how innocent they look. Why, they may have been thieves! Besides, I wanted to get to my destination as soon as possible. I didn't want to have to settle for a room below my station. So, I left them there on the road. I'm sure they made it to Bethlehem, eventually.

(Mary and Joseph enter from back of church)

Reader 2: By the time Mary and Joseph reached Bethlehem, they were hungry, dusty, tired, and in desperate need of a place to stay. The streets were clogged with people. Vainly, they went from inn to inn in search of a bed and a meal. Mary kept up a good front, but Joseph could see the strain in her eyes. She was due to have the baby any day now; he had to find a place for her to rest! Joseph's worry grew to near panic as innkeeper after innkeeper informed them that there was no room available.

(As Mary and Joseph approach the front of the church, the Innkeeper and Innkeeper's Wife meet them at the center of the communion rail)

Joseph had almost given up when they came to an inn on the edge of town. The innkeeper repeated the phrase that Joseph had heard so many times — "No Room."

(Joseph, Mary, Innkeeper, and Innkeeper's wife pantomime the conversation as the Reader continues)

The usually quiet carpenter could not stand any more. Mary hadn't complained, but he could see how tired she was.

"There must be something!" he argued. "My wife is expecting, and the journey has been so hard on her!"

The innkeeper's wife could see that Mary's time was near. She could see how uncomfortable Mary was. "What about the stable?" she asked her husband. "It's not much, but it is clean and warm."

Joseph readily agreed. The innkeeper's wife gave them some blankets, and her husband showed Mary and Joseph to the stable.

(Innkeeper leads Mary and Joseph to the manger which should be situated centrally, near the altar, and then leaves. Joseph should place a blanket around Mary's shoulders as she kneels on one side of the manger. Joseph should then kneel at the other side)

Innkeeper: That was quite a time! Thanks to Caesar's census, all of Judea was on the move, and in need of a place to stay. I wonder if Caesar knew what a big favor he did for us innkeepers? We had people sleeping three and four to a bed! All of them paid full price, too!

I don't know if I saw Mary and Joseph from Nazareth or not. There were so many people that we had to turn many away. Their faces all melted together, if you know what I mean. Believe me, if I could have squeezed them in, I would have. I never turn my back on money if I can avoid it. But we did turn a lot of people away in the days of census. I hated to do it, but we had no choice. You can only fit so many people into one building.

I may have seen the young couple from Nazareth; I don't know. Like I said, after a while, they all looked alike to me.

Music *(soprano or alto solo)*   "Sweet Little Jesus Boy"

(Mary takes the baby from hiding, cuddles it, and then lays it in the manger)

Reader 3: Later that night, the silence of the Judean plain was pierced by a baby's first cry. The Son of God, the Savior of all humankind, was lovingly and tenderly wrapped in swaddling cloths and laid in a manger.

Joseph looked with wonder at his new foster child. Would he be up to the great task that God had given him? He was only a simple carpenter. What if he makes mistakes raising God's Son?

But Mary's heart was at peace. It was a peace that she had known since the angel had spoken to her nine months before. Her face glowed with love as she looked down at her sleeping son, and then up into her husband's eyes.

Music *(soprano or alto solo)* "Ave Maria"

(During the song, the Shepherds enter from the back of the sanctuary and proceed up the center aisle to the communion rail, where they pantomime with the Angels as their story is read)

Reader 4: As Mary and Joseph shared that holy silence, shepherds, watching over their flocks, were startled by a bright light *(Angels enter from right)* and a voice from heaven. They covered their faces and shook with fear. But the voice was gentle.

"Don't be afraid," it said.

The shepherds looked up and saw an angel in white robes standing in front of them. And just beyond, a host of angels sang God's praises to the sky.

"I bring you good tidings of great joy, which shall be to all people," the angel said. "For unto you is born this day, in the City of David, a Savior, which is Christ the Lord. And this shall be a sign unto you; you shall find the babe wrapped in swaddling cloths, and lying in a manger." Then all the angels joined in singing, "Glory to God in the highest, and on earth, peace, and good will toward all men!"

(Angels exit to stand behind the manger. Shepherds kneel in front of manger)

Reader 5: When the angels had ascended, the shepherds left their flocks and hurried to the stable on the outskirts of Bethlehem. When they got there, they saw Mary and Joseph, and the baby sleeping in the manger, just as the angels had said that they would. This was not the way they had expected the Messiah to come to them. The surroundings were humble, but they fell on their knees at the sight of him, and worshiped their newborn King.

Later, three kings from the East would do the same, but on that holiest of nights, it was a few simple shepherds that God chose to witness the greatest event of all time: the birth of Jesus Christ.

(The Readers and all the other children, with the exception of Mary, Joseph, and the Shepherds, who maintain their positions, join the Angels to form a half circle behind the manger)

Music *(all participating children)* "Away In The Manger"

(After the song, all the children, except Mary and Joseph, may exit right. Mary and Joseph should maintain their positions on either side of the manger)

Reader 6: The pageant is completed. You see before you the same sight that greeted the shepherds so many years ago: the stable, the manger, the young woman Mary — her face aglow with the special warmth that all new mothers know — Joseph beside her — happy beyond words — and finally the baby, so small, so helpless, lying in a manger.

We are not as lowly as the shepherds, nor as mighty as the kings who bowed low before this tiny child, but we, too, have heard the good news of the angels. We, too, are called upon to put off our worldly pride and kneel in true repentant humility before our infant Savior, singing prayers of thanksgiving, and filled with wonder at the great love our God bears us, that he would sacrifice his only Son for our salvation!

Leader: Come forward now and offer your gifts unto the Lord.

(At this point, the ushers direct the congregation to place their offerings in baskets that are placed on the floor, in front of the manger. Holy Communion may also be administered at this time as the people kneel before the manger)

Offertory *(choir)*   "Oh, Come, All Ye Faithful"

(After all the people have returned to their seats, Mary and Joseph exit)

Prayer *(unison)*

Dear Lord, who gave your only Son for our salvation, fill our hearts with the simple, steadfast love of a child. Keep the spirit of Christmas forever young in our hearts, so that, like shepherds, we may never cease to wonder at thy love. Help us, Father, to come to you today, and enter into the boundless joy that the shepherds felt on that holiest of nights.

In the name of him whose birth we remember today, cleanse our souls, so that we might become as little children. And like the Wise Men, help us to follow your star in our lives forever.

In the name of the Father, and of the Son, and of the Holy Spirit, we pray. Amen.

Music *(choir)*   "Hark! The Herald Angels Sing"

Reader 7: According to the gospel, the shepherds, after they had worshiped their infant Savior, "made known abroad the saying which was told them concerning the child." What a wide variety of responses they must have received to the angels' story! There were many, undoubtedly, who believed and flocked to the stable to worship the King, and to share the joy that the shepherds had received. But there were others who, like so many people today, rejected the good news, and were unable to share that joy.

Merchant: The shepherds? Yes, I heard their story, and the stories of others who visited the stable on the edge of town. I'm told that there were even three kings from the East who visited the young couple from Nazareth and their infant son. But the whole thing is just too fantastic to believe! The Son of God born in a stable? Surely, if God were to send his Son to earth in the form of a baby, he would be born to a king or a priest, not a carpenter, and especially not one from Nazareth, of all places! I simply cannot believe that this child lying in a manger was the Son of the Almighty God.

Not that I wasn't curious. The child must have been remarkable, since so many who did go to see him came away believing that he was the Messiah. Oh, yes, I was curious, but not curious enough to go to that dirty stable myself. I mean, what if the word got out that I, a respected member of the community, listened to the rantings of a bunch of star-struck shepherds?

No, I didn't go to see him. It wasn't worth the risk. A man's reputation is precious. I wasn't about to risk mine on the basis of such a fantastic tale. Angels talking to shepherds! A king born in a stable! Ridiculous!

Reader 8: And so it began on that holy night so long ago. A baby was born in a stable, a baby that 33 short years later would suffer the pain and humiliation of death on a cross to offer us the gift of salvation.

The story is fantastic. It seems inconceivable that one small child could have such power. But, it is even more fantastic that God loves us so much that he would give his only Son as a sacrifice for our sin.

The choice is ours now. Do we walk comfortably away, wrapped in the security of intellect and propriety? Or, do we, like the shepherds, throw off the things of this world, and embrace our Lord, our King, our Savior, Jesus Christ? Choose now. Choose life. Choose Christ! Come share the joy by joining us in song!

Congregational Hymn   "Joy To The World"

Benediction

Postlude

Director's Notes

Director's Notes

Contributors

Anne W. Anderson is a free-lance writer who regularly contributes to *Pockets* magazine for children. She also works for United Methodist Cooperative Ministries in Clearwater, Florida. Anderson is her congregation's drama director and writes much of the material they perform. She also serves as a Sunday school teacher and choir member.

Nelson Chamberlain is the pastor of Zion Congregational Church in Brighton, Colorado. Prior to entering the ministry, he served for several years at Presbyterian Children's Ministry in Texas. Chamberlain is a graduate of Houghton College, the University of Texas-Arlington, and Dallas Theological Seminary.

Linda Buff is a former high school biology teacher who currently is a Sunday school teacher and Bible study leader at Northwood Presbyterian Church in Spokane, Washington. She is a graduate of the University of California-San Diego and California State University-Bakersfield.

Sharon Cathcart is an obstetrician and gynecologist in private practice, who also serves as a Sunday school teacher at Northwood Presbyterian Church in Spokane, Washington. She is a graduate of St. Olaf College and Chicago College of Osteopathic Medicine.

Pamela Honan Peterson is the author of numerous church school curriculum courses for Augsburg Fortress and more than 250 articles in various Christian magazines. She is currently the director of Christian education at First Presbyterian Church in Mishawaka, Indiana. Peterson is a graduate of Wittenberg University and the Lutheran School of Theology at Chicago.

J. B. Quisenberry has written and directed chancel dramas (several published by CSS) for more than thirty years. She is an active member of Grace United Methodist Church in Elgin Illinois, where both she and her husband serve as lay preachers. Quisenberry majored in theater and theology at Luther College and Elgin Community College.